AF256010

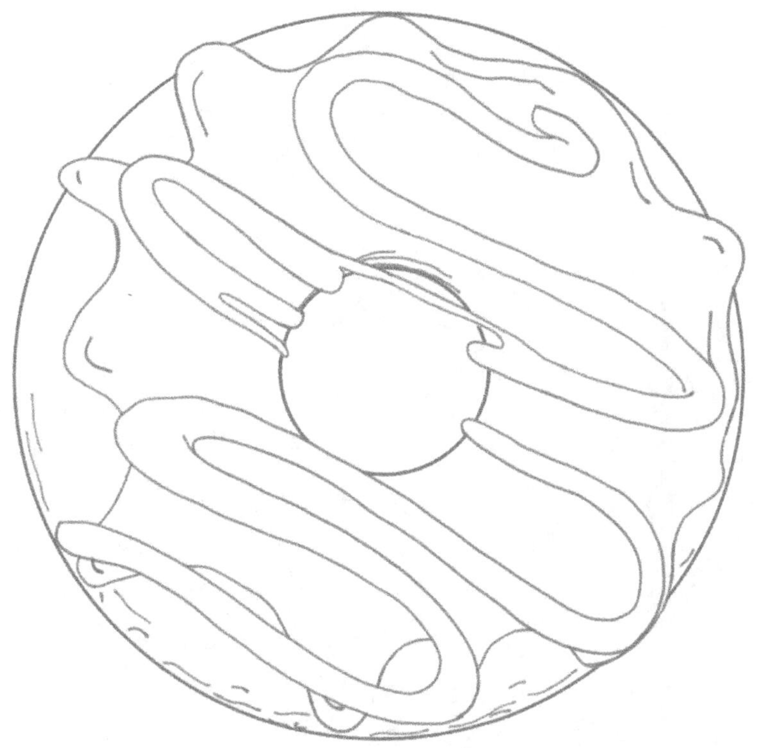

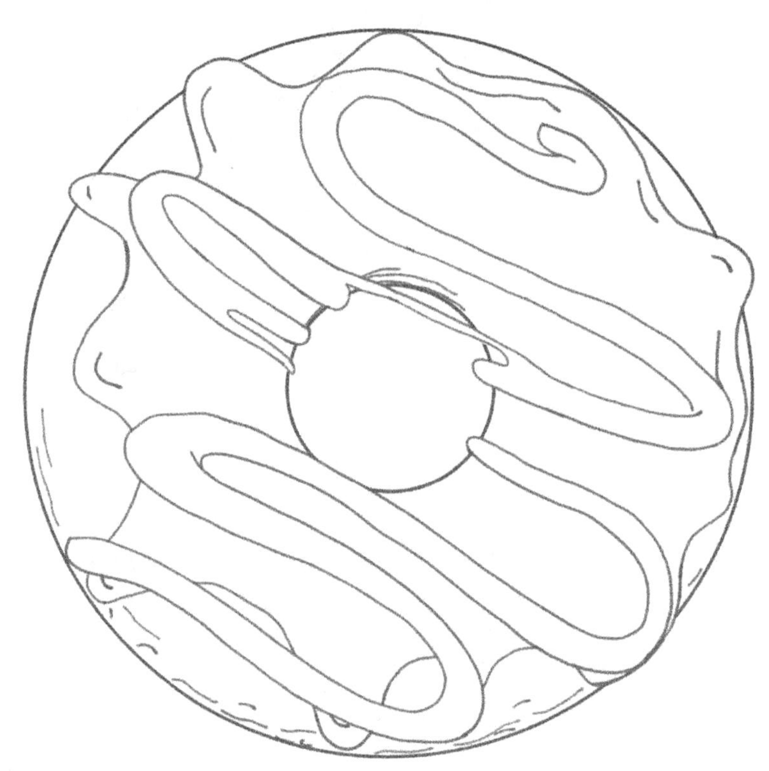

FINISH THE DRAWING

Volume Three

FACES

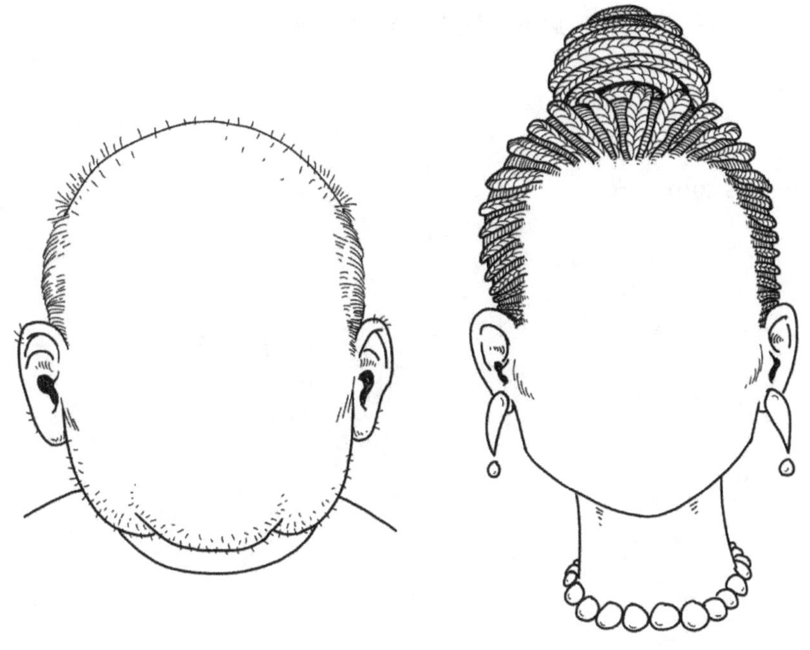

BY

JESS ERSKINE

Finish the Drawing, Volume Three - Faces
Copyright © 2019 Jess Erskine. All Rights Reserved.

No portion of this book may be reproduced - mechanically, electronically,
or by any means whatsoever: including photocopying -
without written permission from the publisher, except in the case of brief
quotations embodied in critical articles and reviews.

Are you a teacher?
Want to use our Finish the Drawing series in your classroom?
Visit our store at: www.teacherspayteachers.com/Store/Rolling-Donut-Press
For high quality printables with reproduction rights.

If you have any questions or comments, please feel free to reach us by email:
rollingdonutpress@gmail.com

All images are created by, and are the property of Jess Erskine.

Rolling Donut Press
Kentucky, USA

www.RollingDonutPress.com

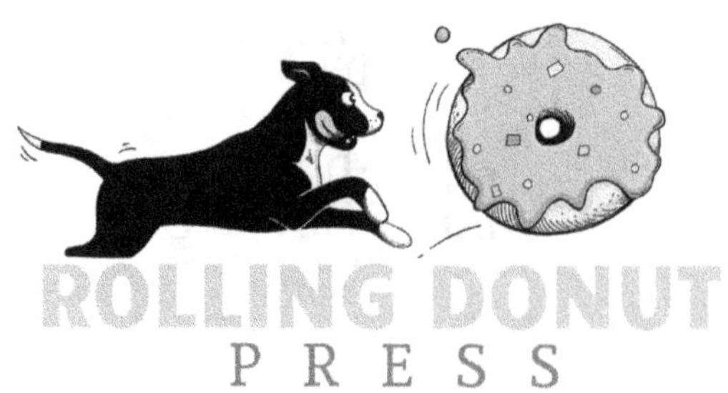

How it works

→ HALF DRAWINGS

Each drawing is half finished to give you a place to start:

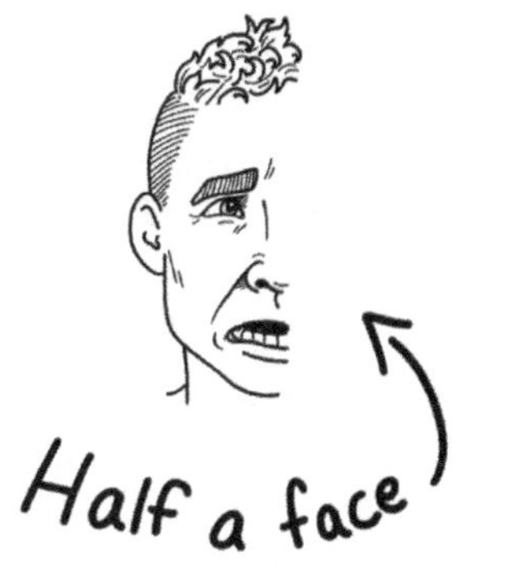

Half a face

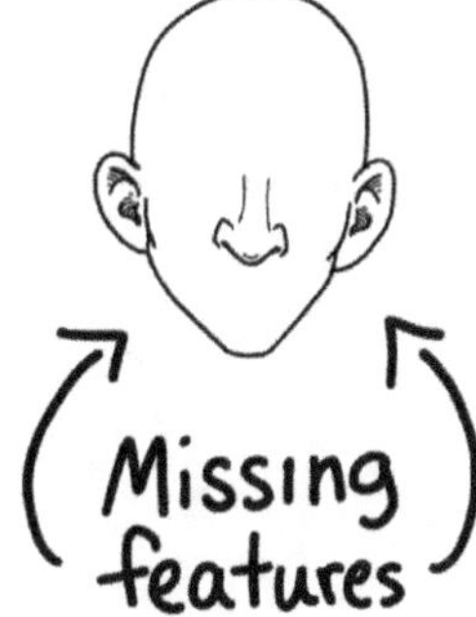

Missing features

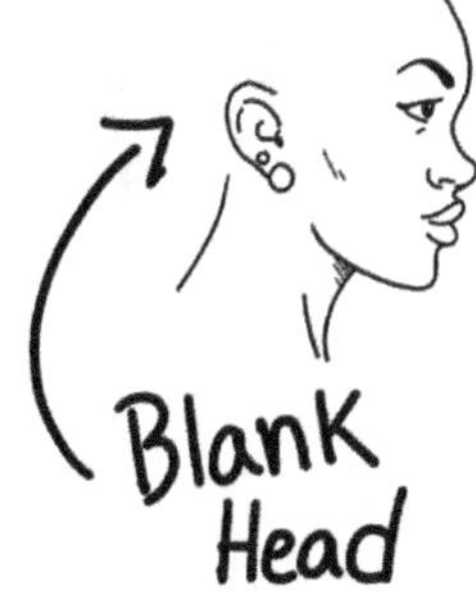

Blank Head

→ THINK OUTSIDE THE BOX

Let your imagination run wild:

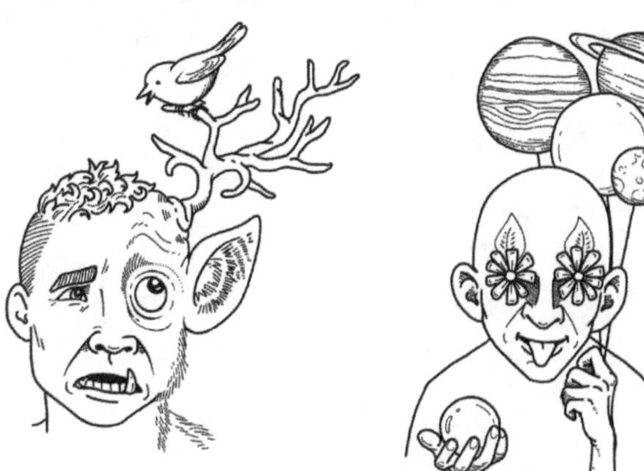

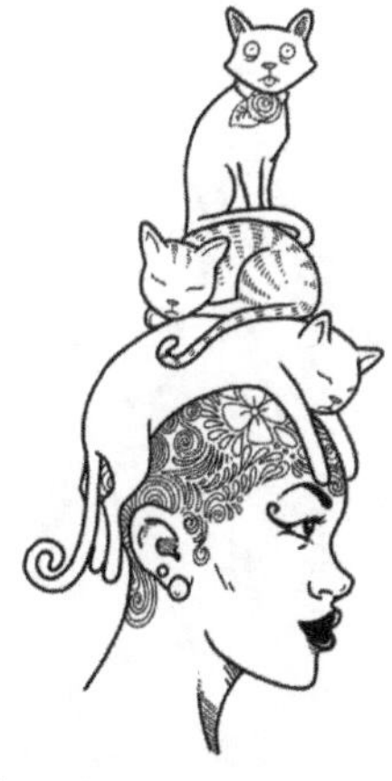

DRAW SILLY

It doesn't have to match!

DRAW CREATIVE

Put unexpected combinations together!

JUST DRAW!

What ever you want however you want!

CREATIVE JUICE RUNNING ON EMPTY?

 TAKE A WALK OUTSIDE 

 DO SOMETHING ELSE FOR AWHILE 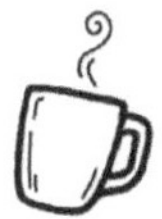

OR

CHECK OUT THE IDEA KEYS FOR SOME QUICK INSPIRATION:

- Aliens
- Villians
- Barbarians
- Monsters
- The undead
- Superheroes
- Hipster

- Steampunk
- Medieval
- 1920's style
- Victorian
- Magical
- Comic book style

- Night terrors
- Circus

- Circus
- Big hair
- Hats:
    feathered
    bowler
    derby
    big, tiny
    floral
- Funky jewelry
- Masks
- Silly glasses
- Gawdy makeup
- Tattoos
- Braids + gems
- Exaggerated features
- Age mash-up
- Lots of eyeballs

- Seasonal
- Halloween
- Winter
- Elements

- Sea creatures
- Moths + beetles
- Vines
- Feathers
- Woodland creatures
- Underwater
- Birds + insects
- Floral designs
- Bones + decay
- Cracks
- Crazy colors
- Space

- Expressions:
    sleepy
    sad, angry
    fearful
    happy

- Surrealism
- Geometric shapes
- Time
- Patterns
- Wrinkly material
- Lightbulb + wires
- Swirls
- Stitching + patchwork
- Blocks
- Netting
- Balloons + clouds

QUICK NOTE:

The purpose of Finish the Drawing is to simply get your creativity flowing and to have fun. Don't be discouraged or frustrated with yourself if you're not feeling creative right away, creativity is like a muscle that needs to stretch and grow.
Be good to yourself and enjoy the process!

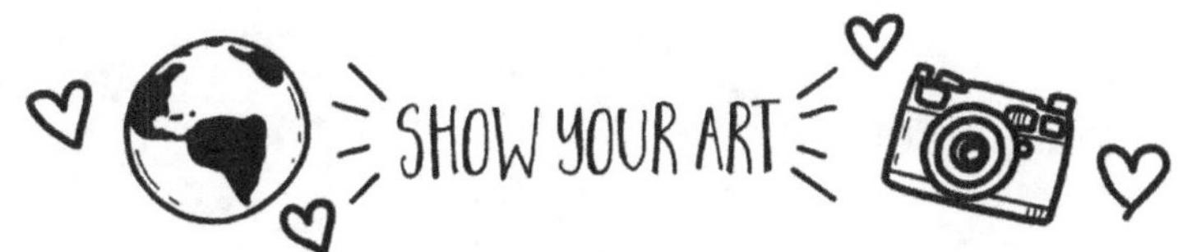

We would love to see your finished drawing and share it on our website!
On instagram tag us: @rollingdonutpress or use the hashtag: #FinishTheDrawingBook
or email us at: rollingdonutpress@gmail.com

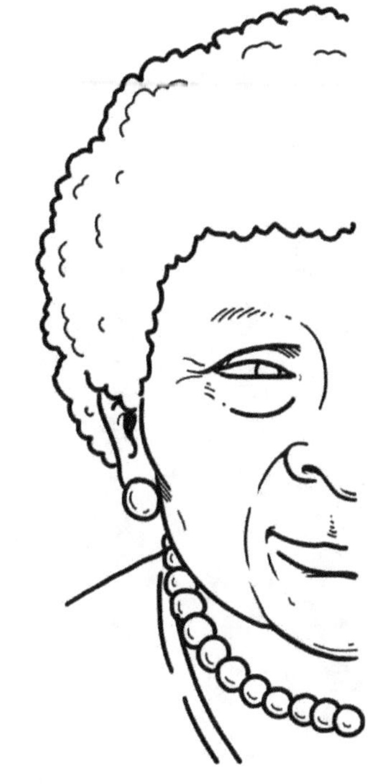

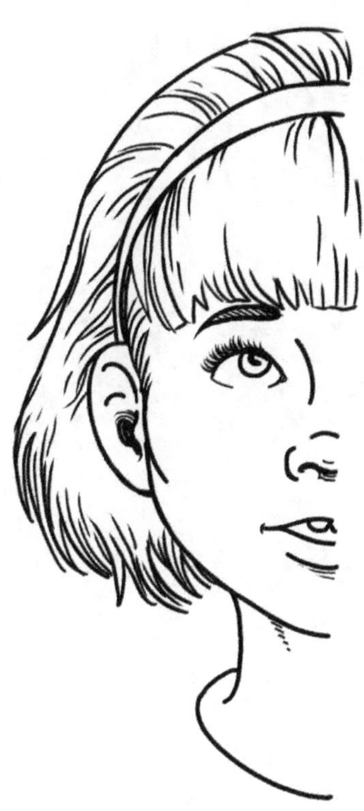

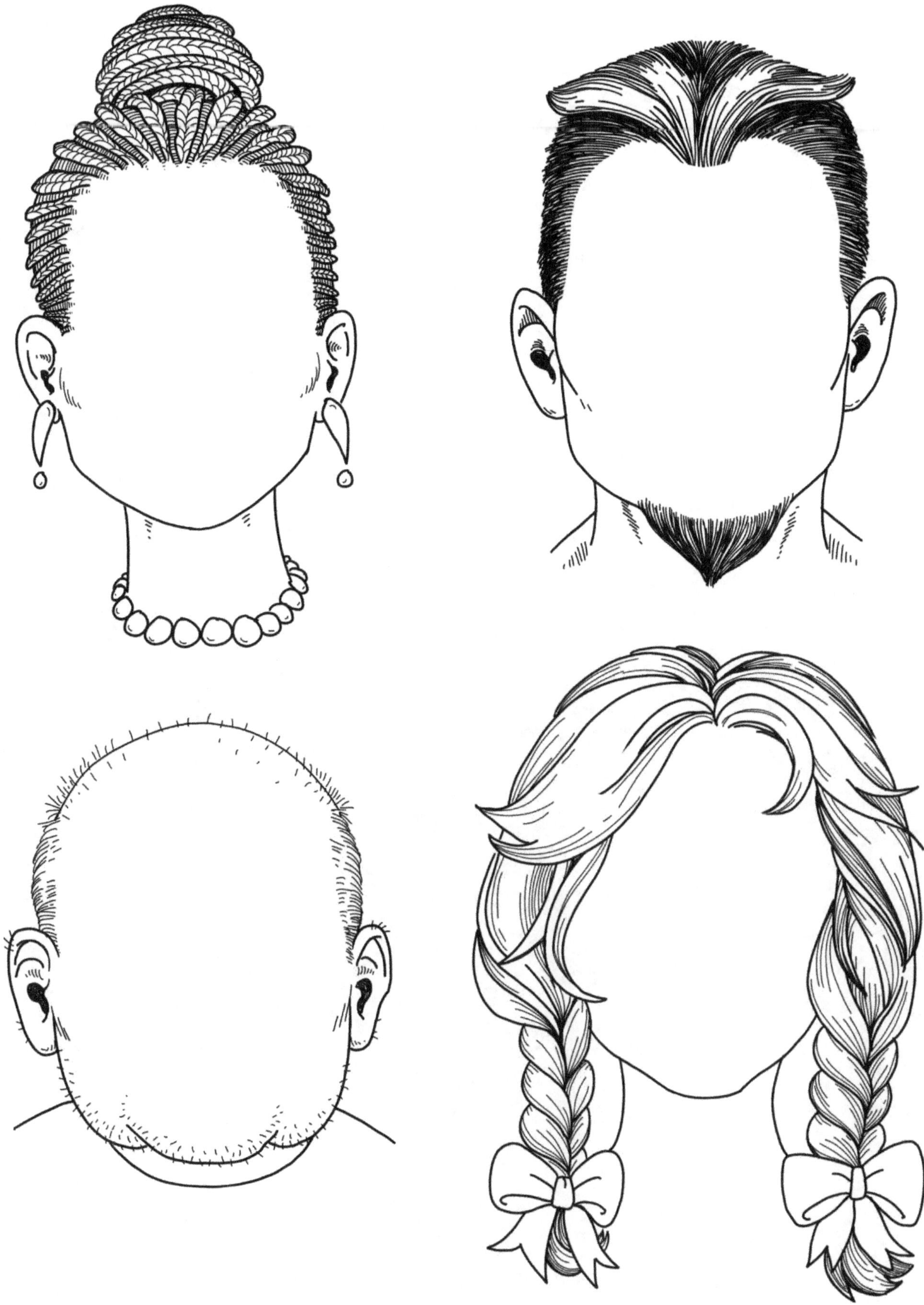

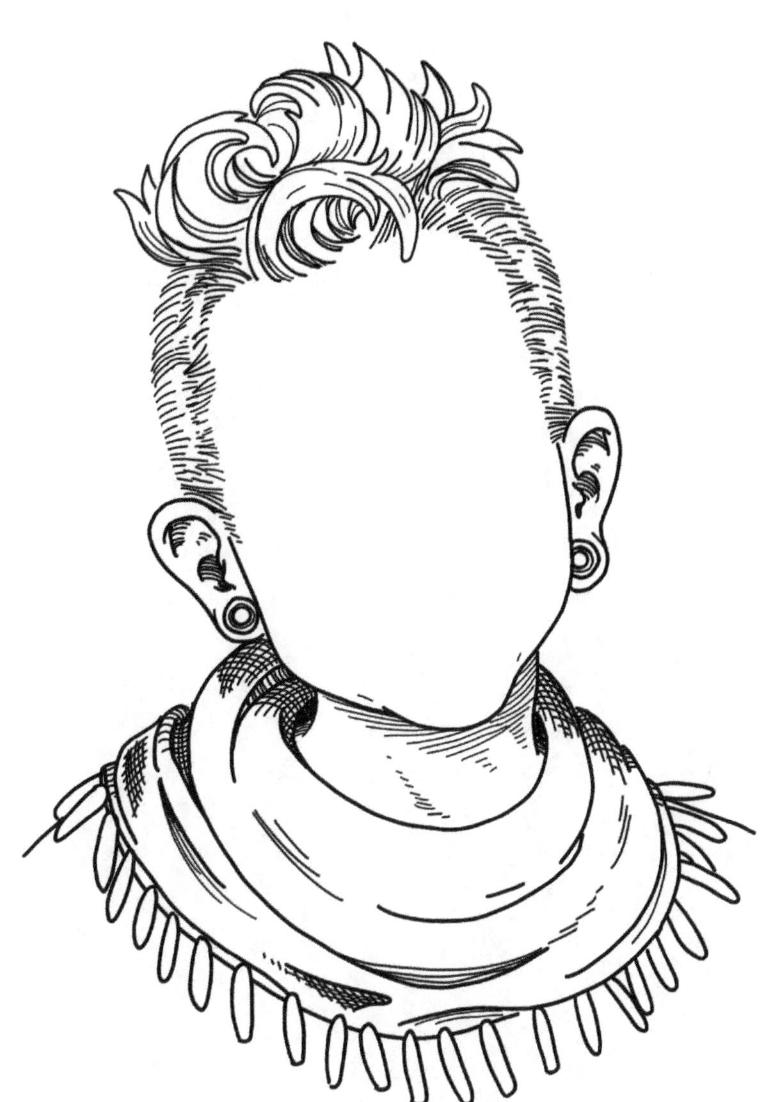

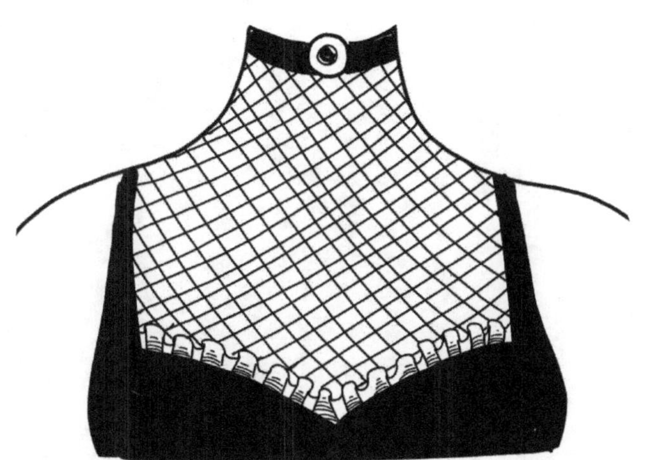
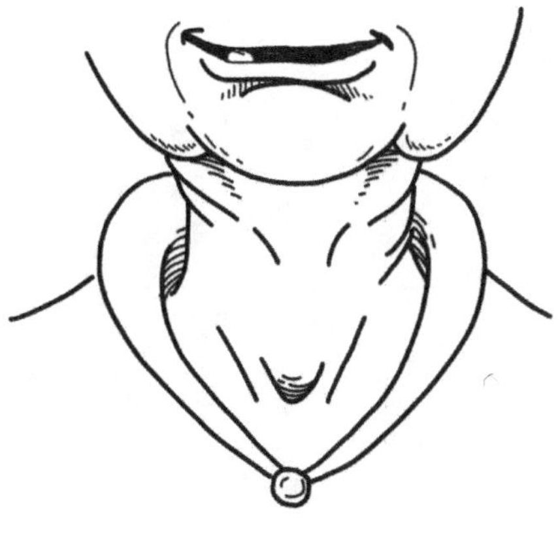

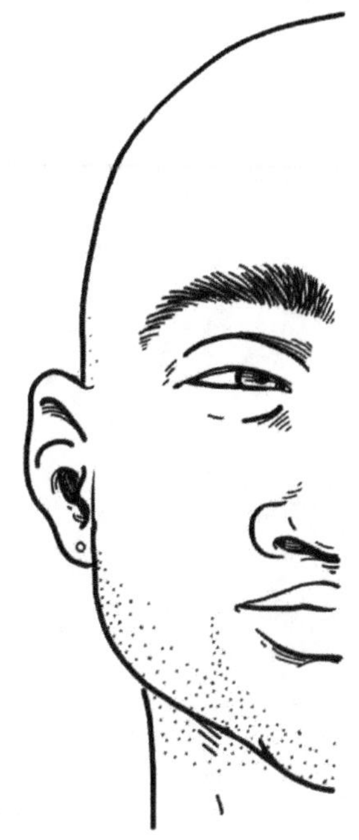

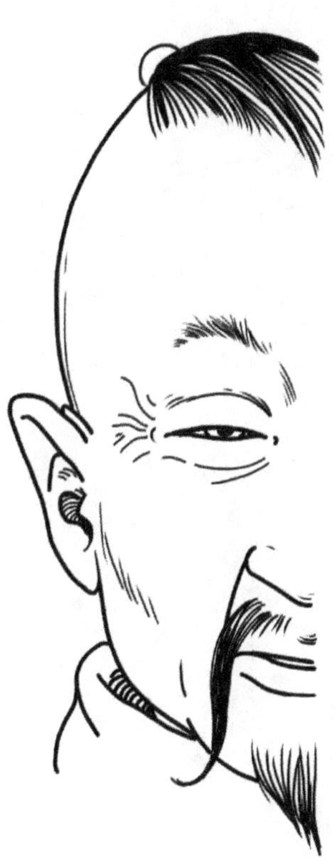

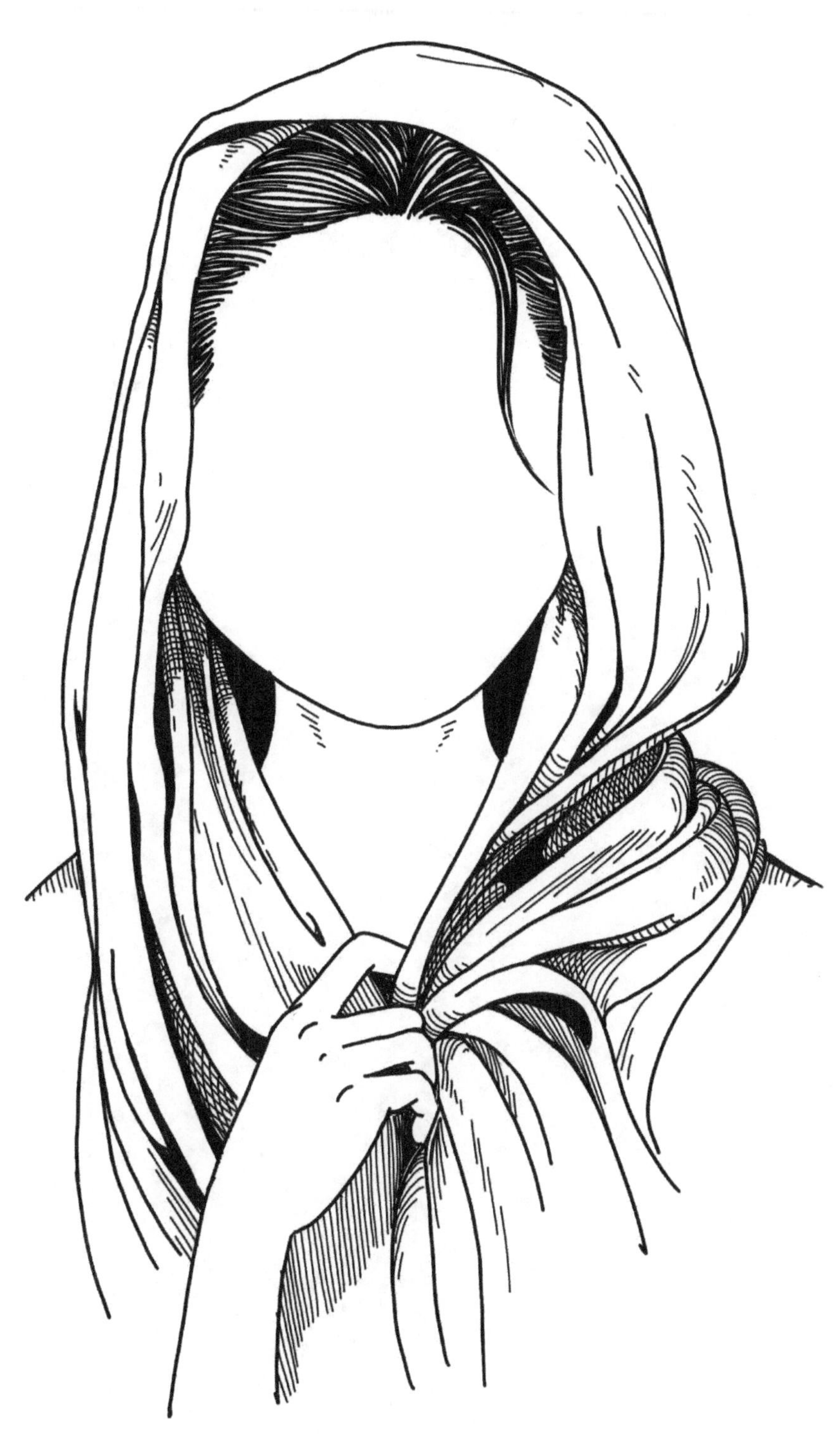

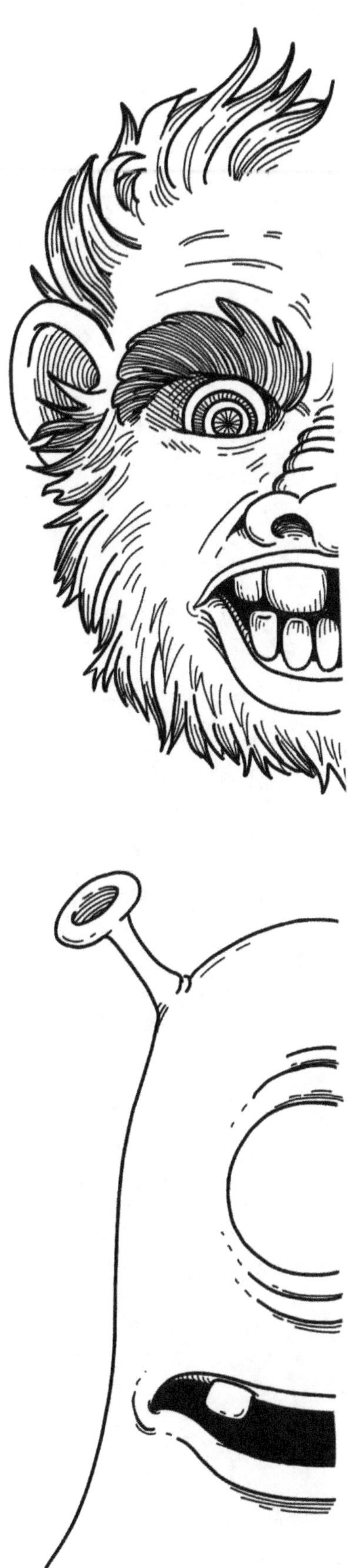

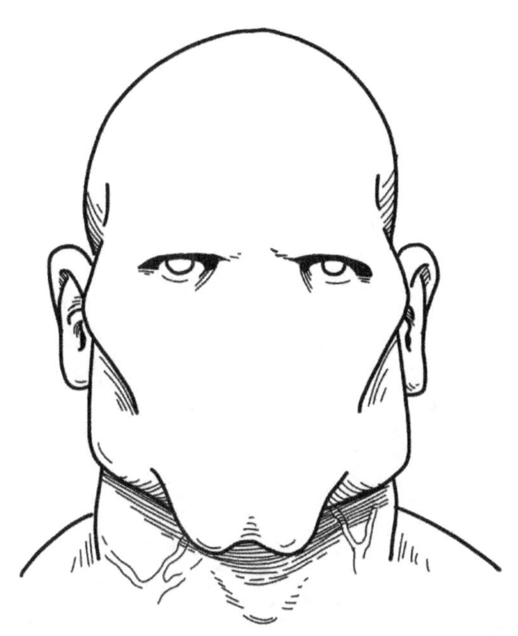
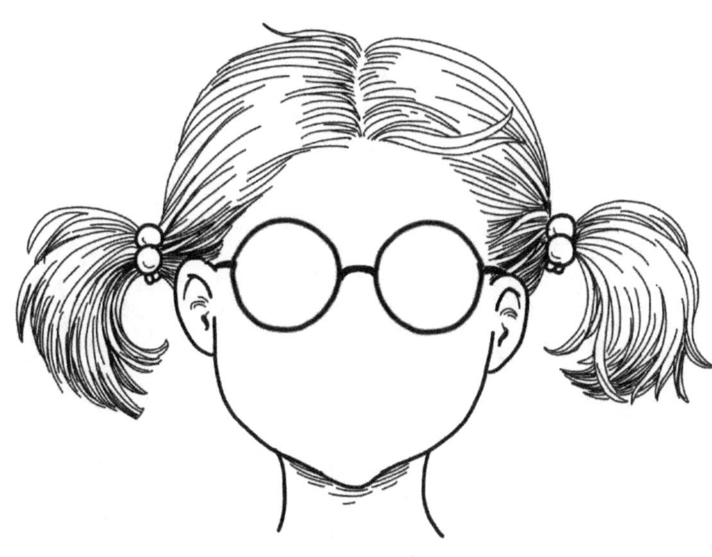

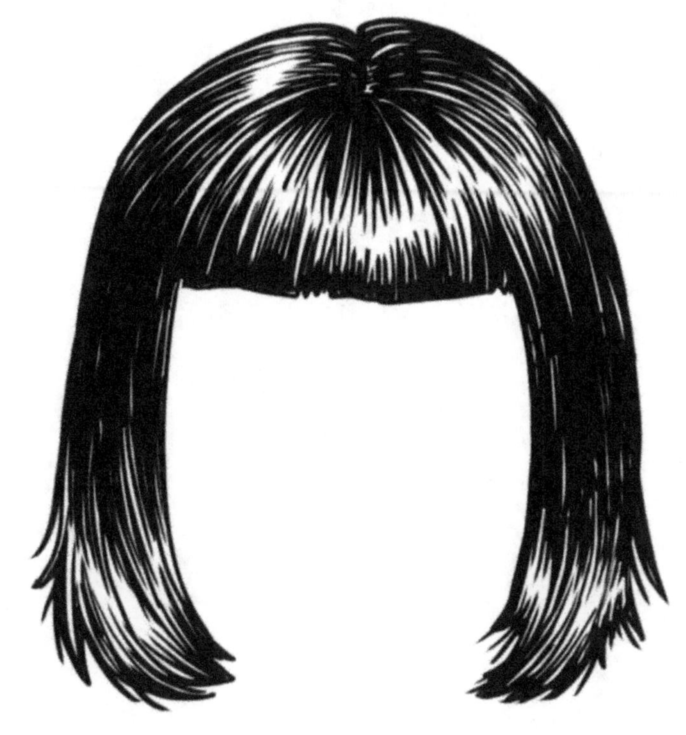

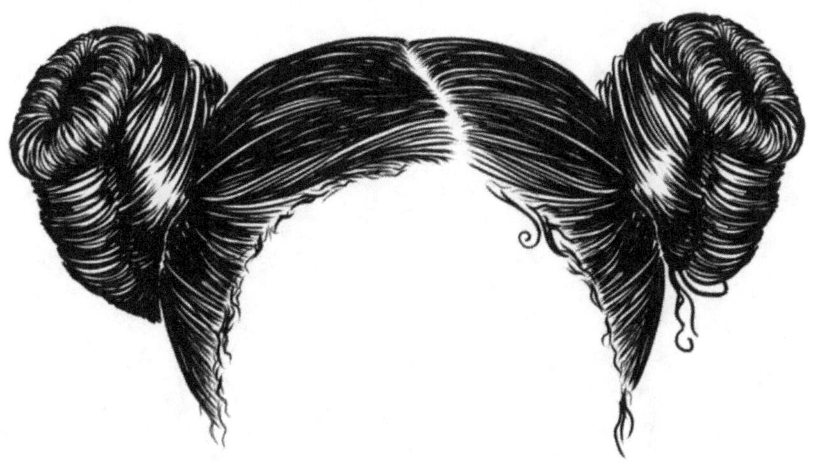

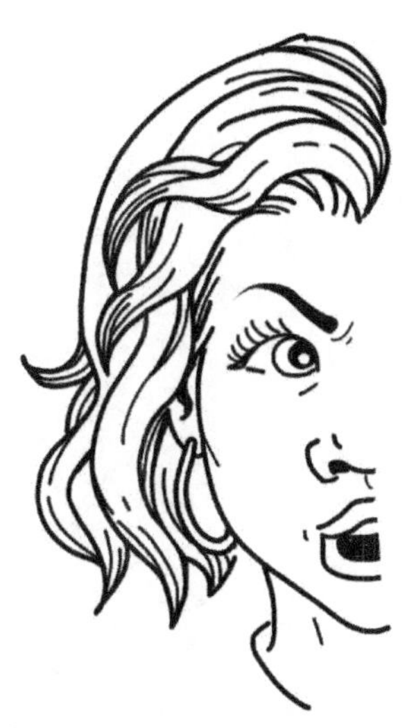

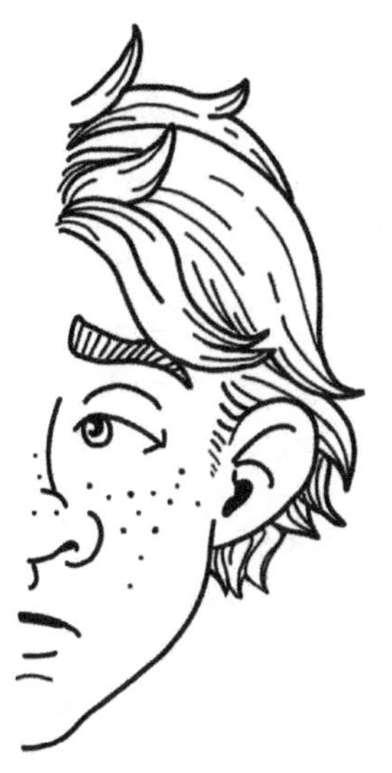

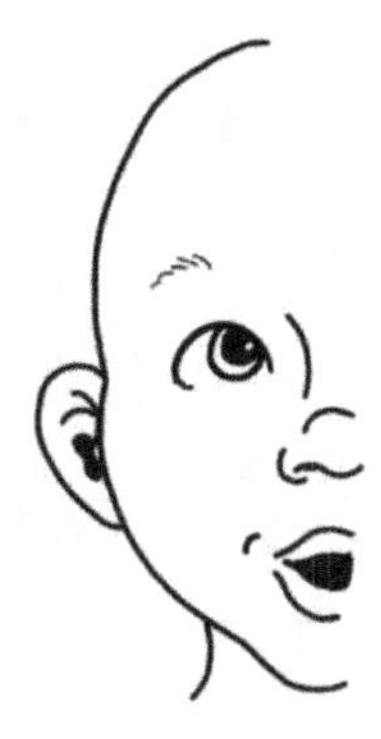

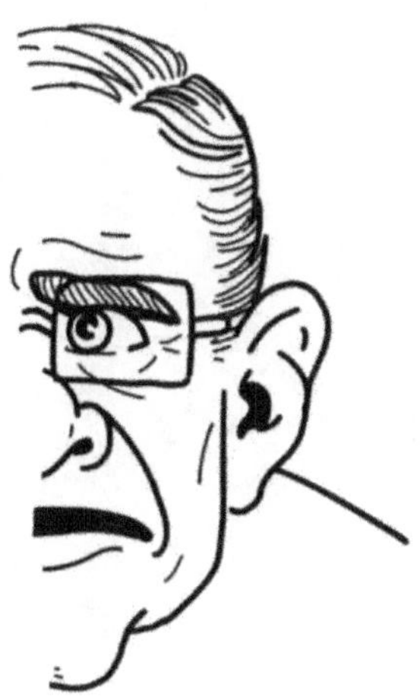

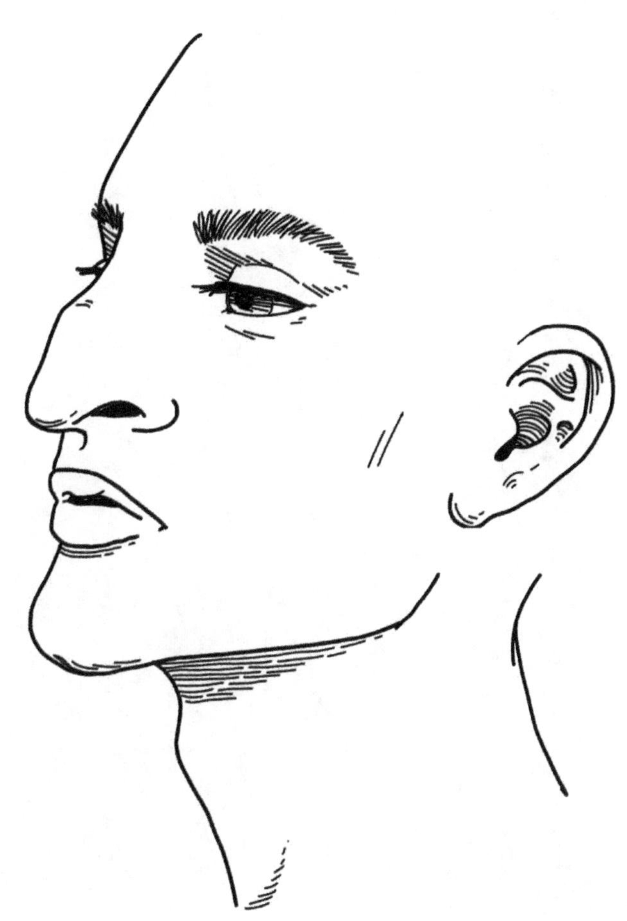

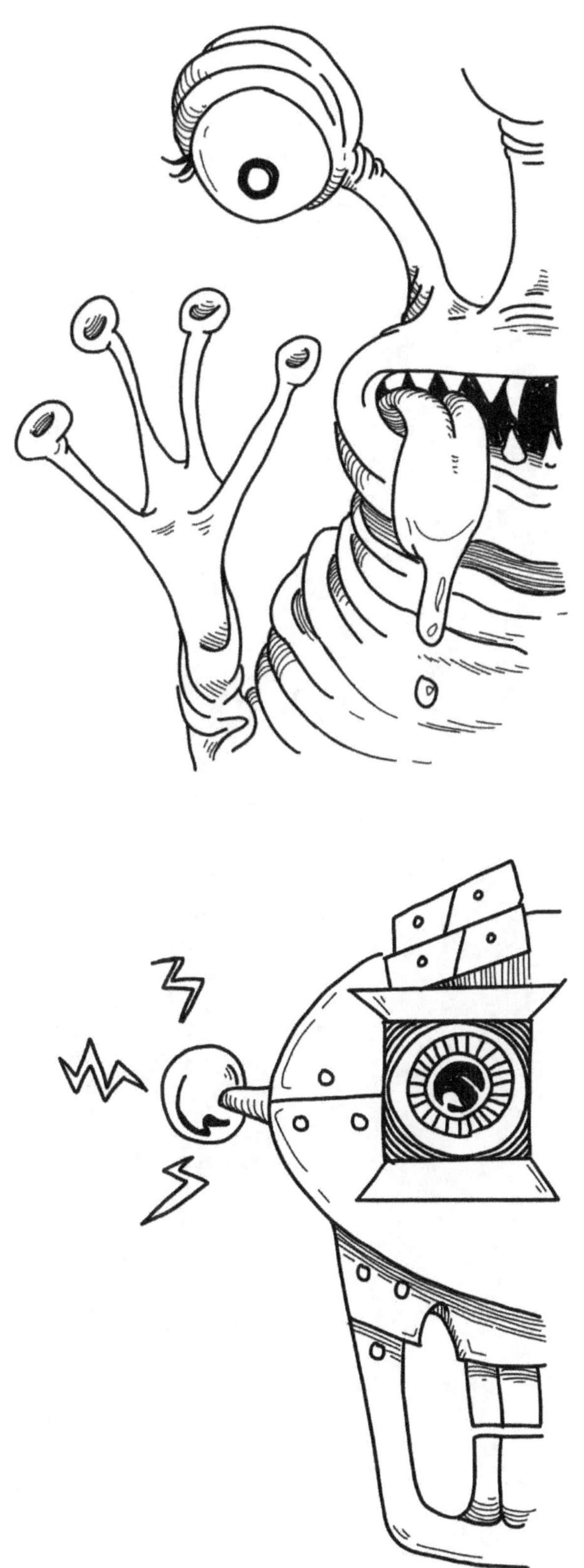

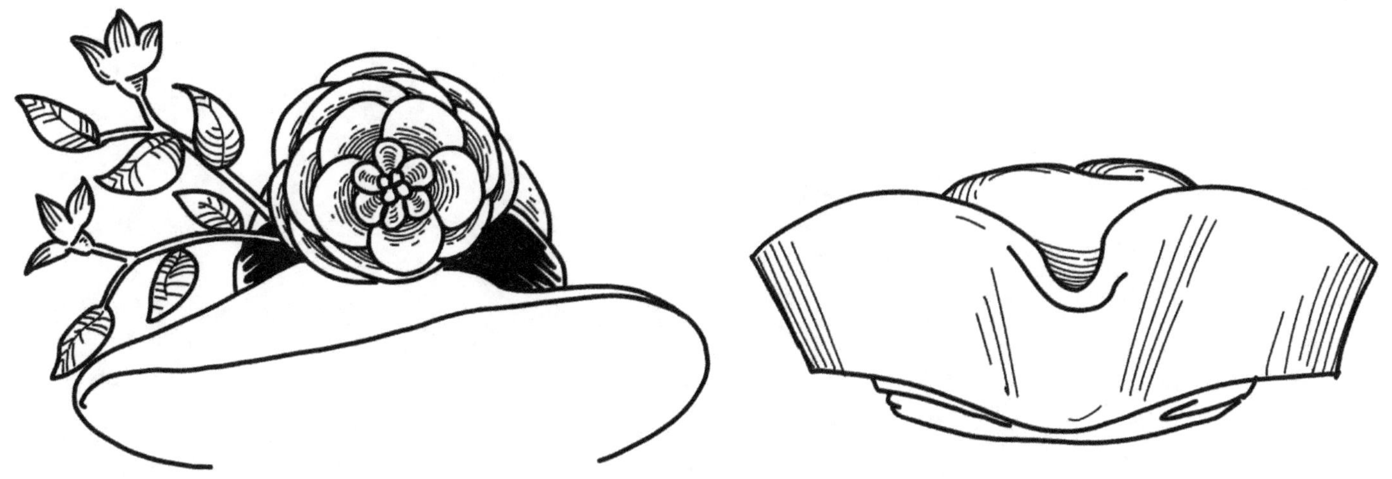

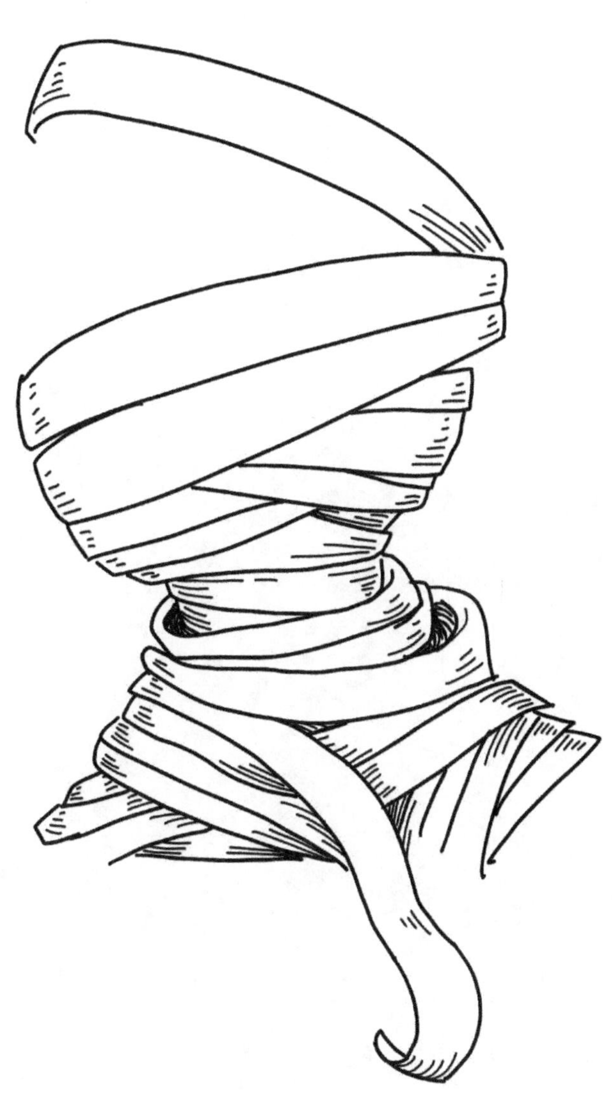

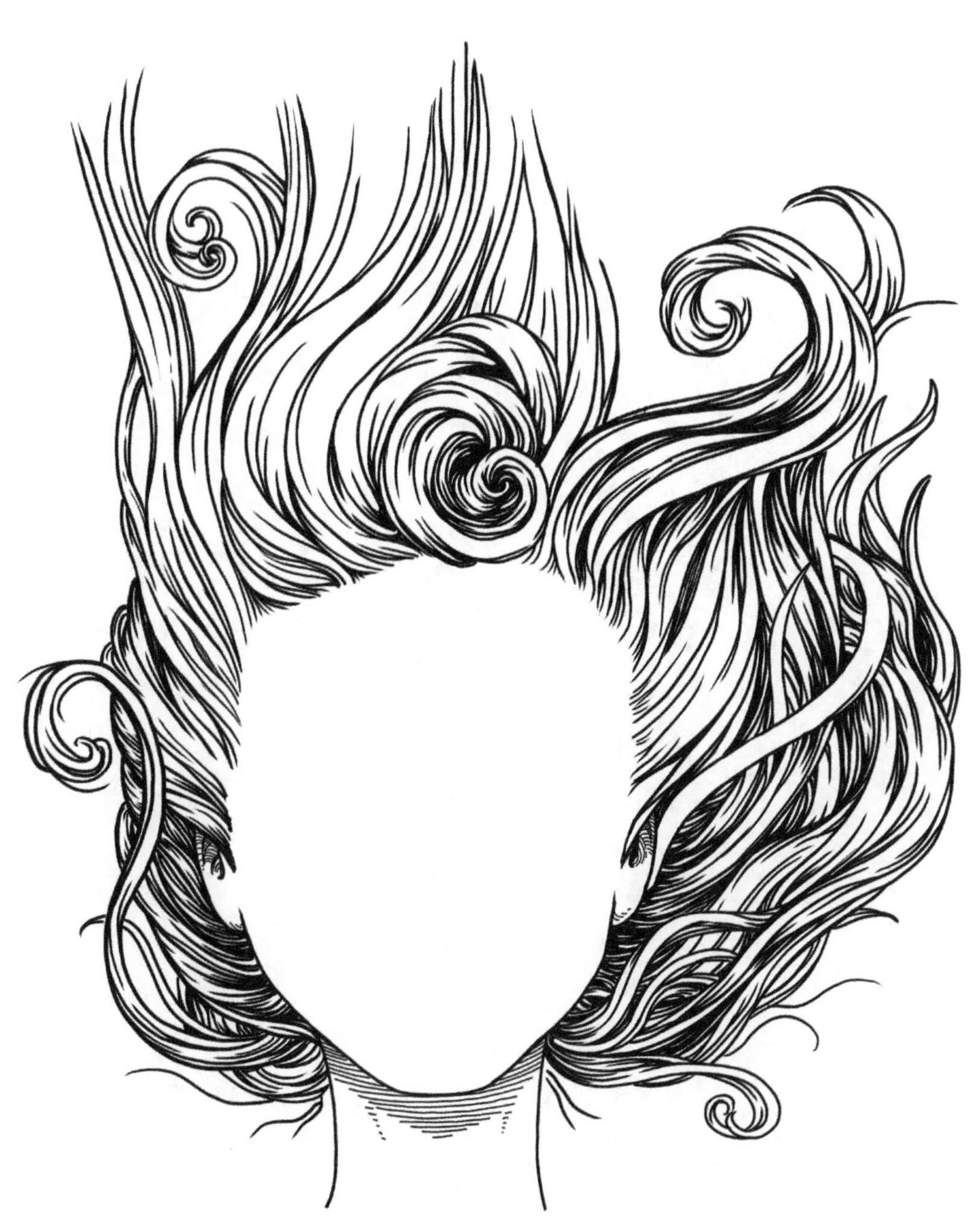

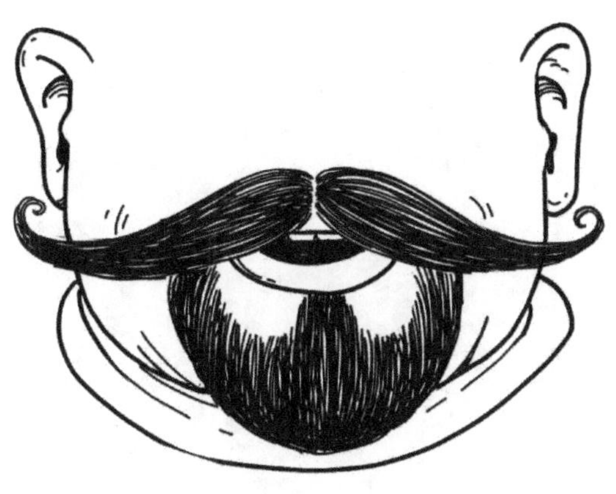
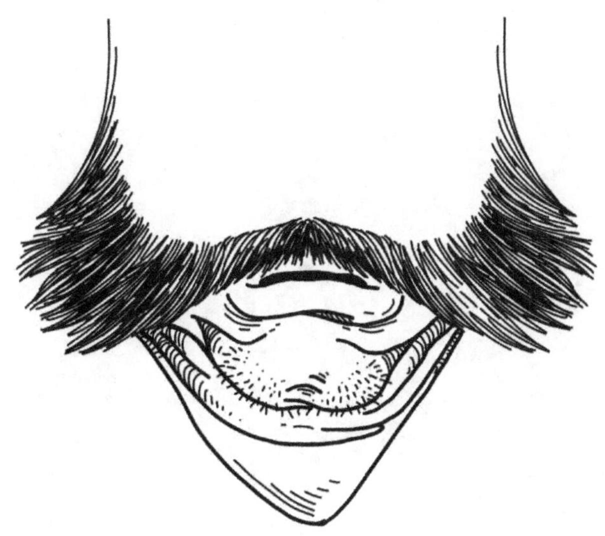

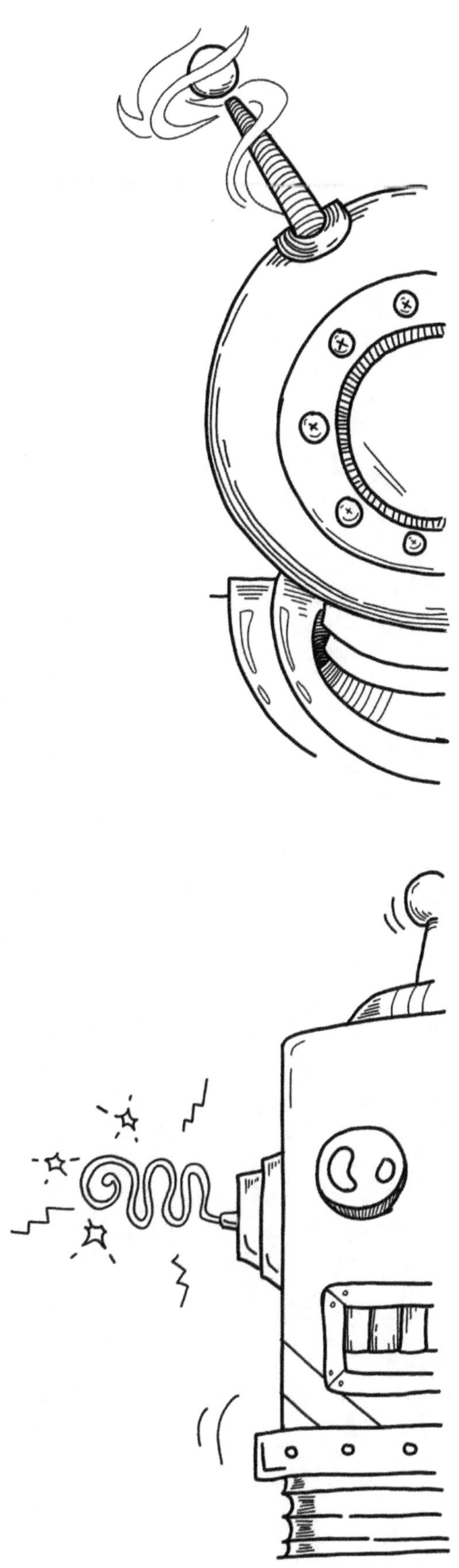

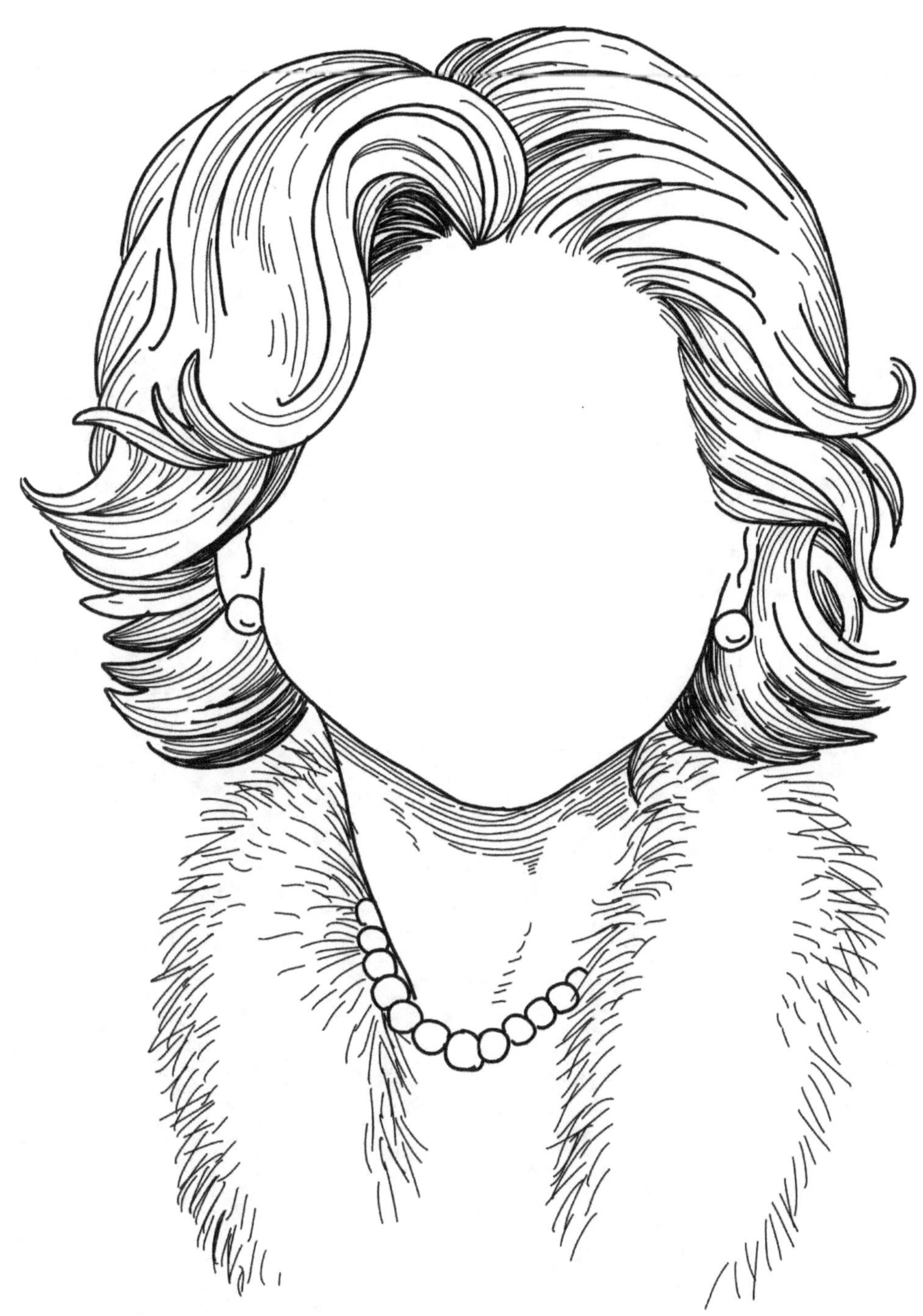

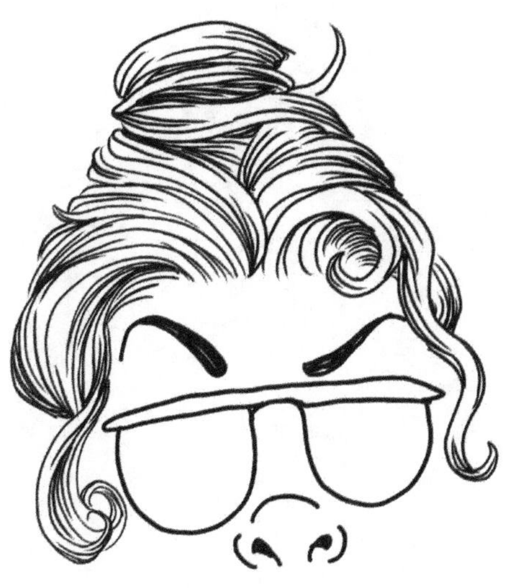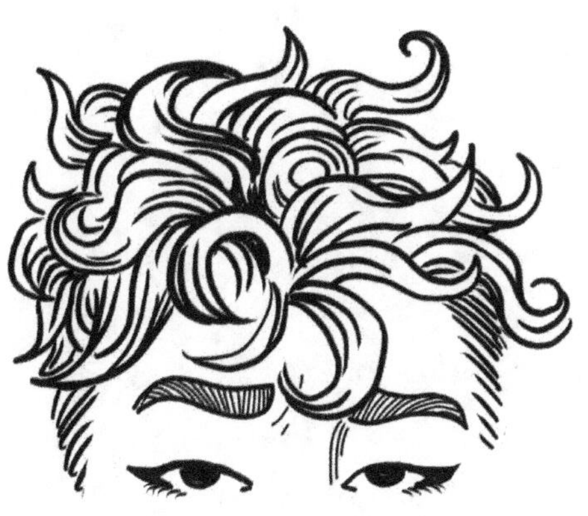

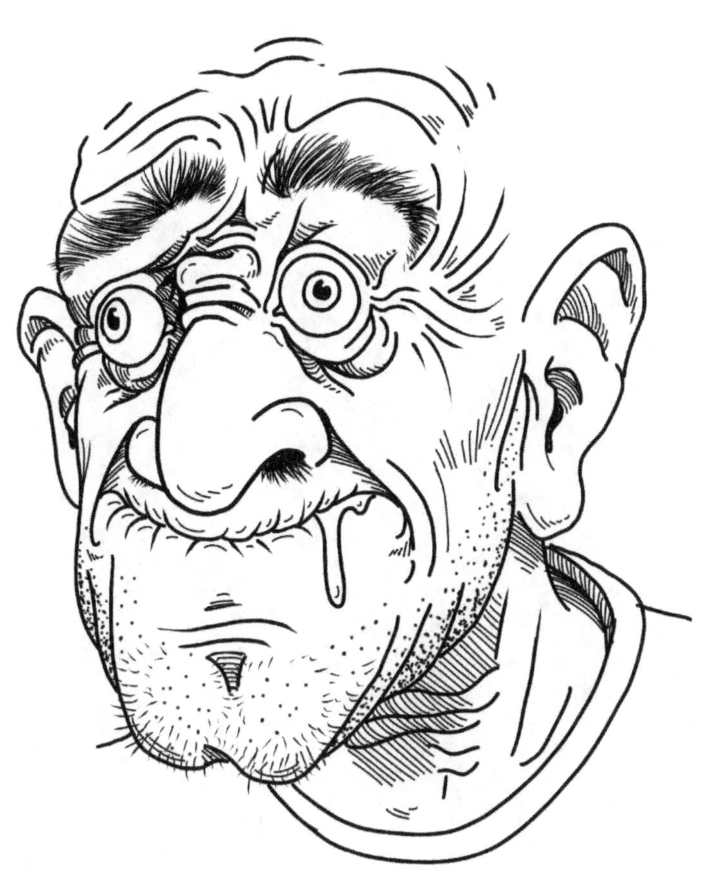

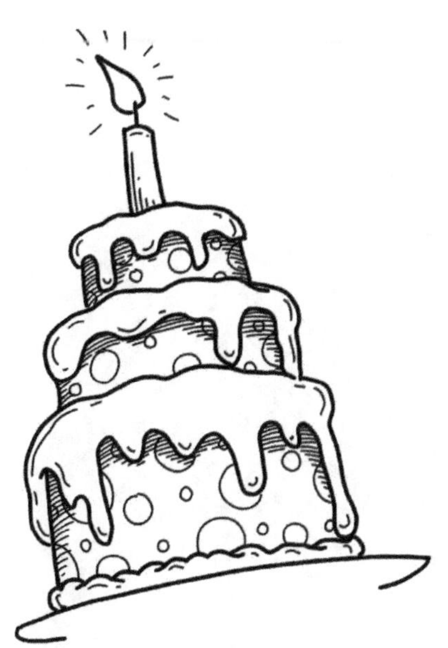

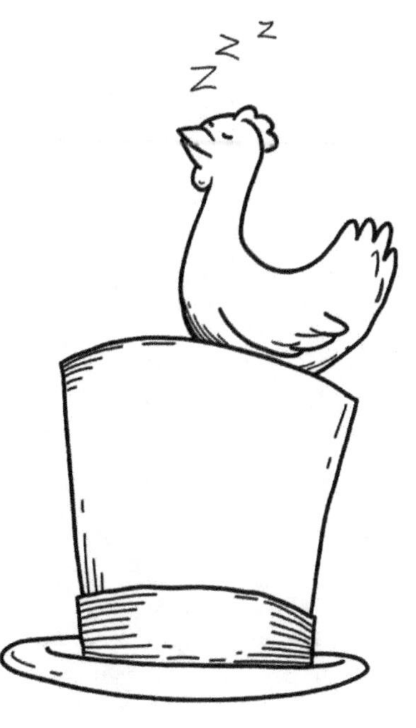

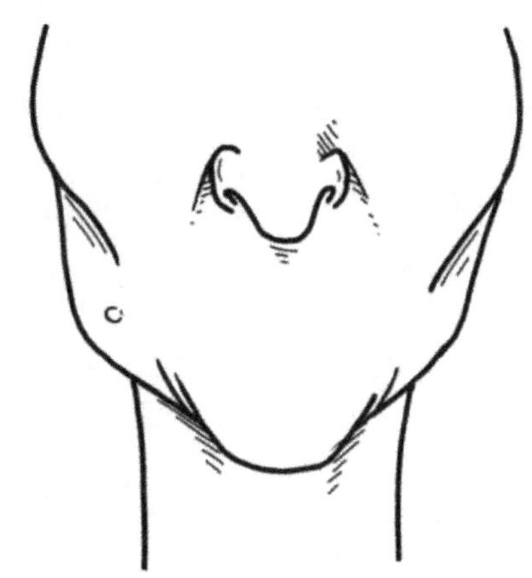
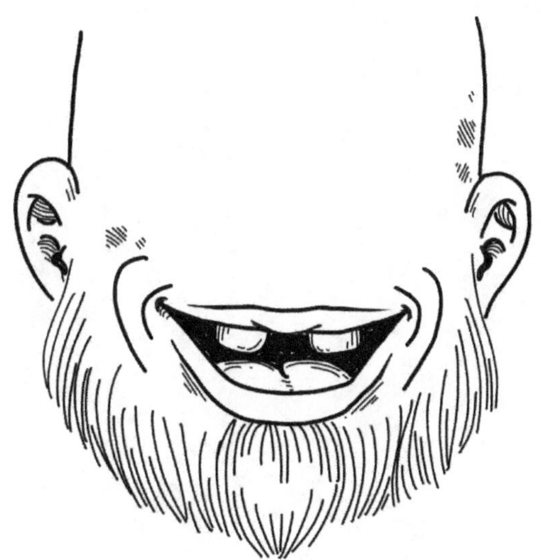

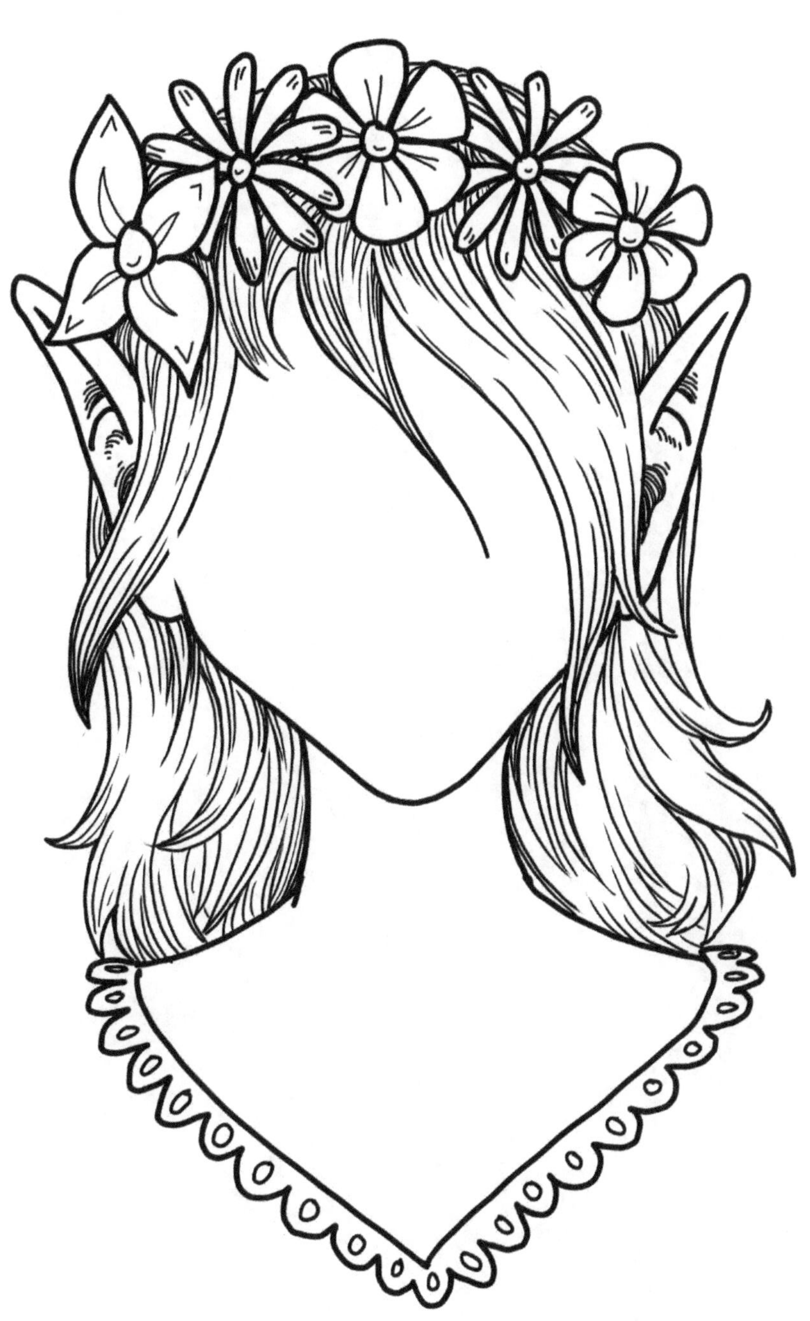

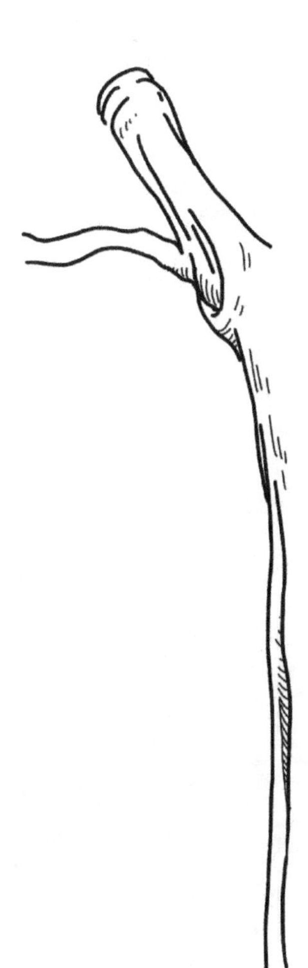

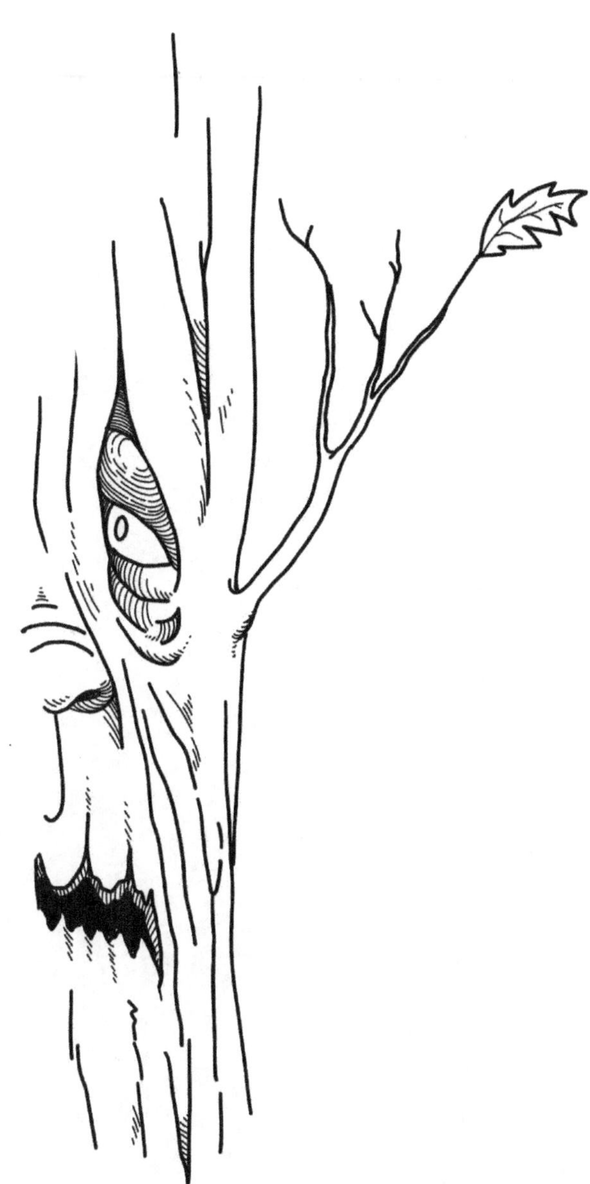

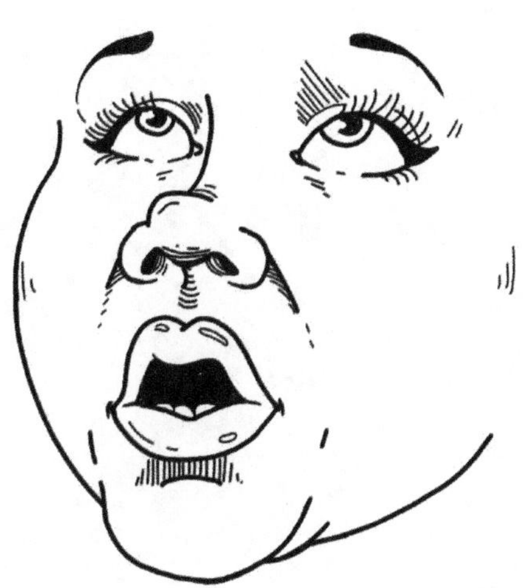

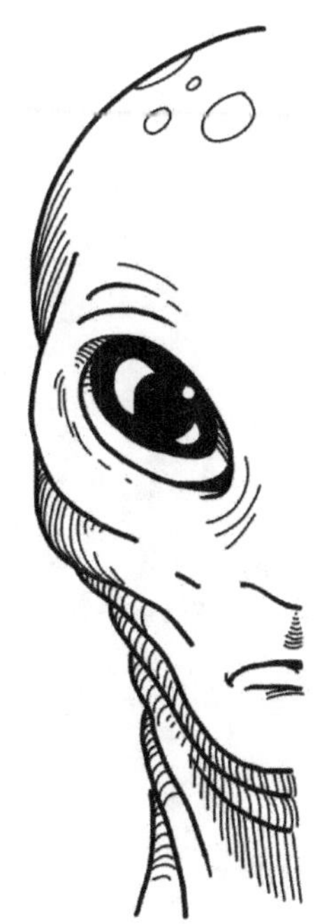

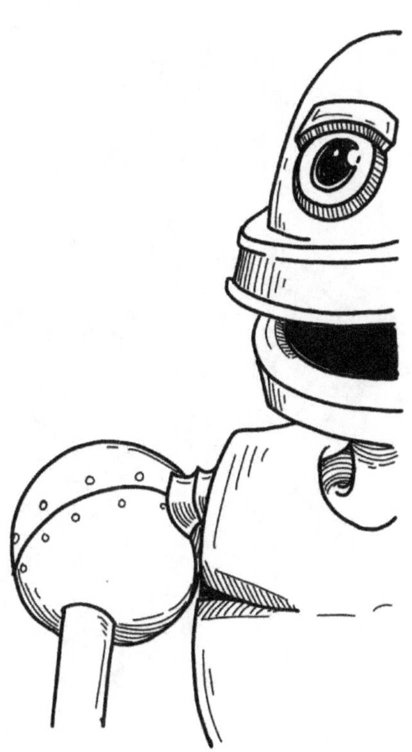

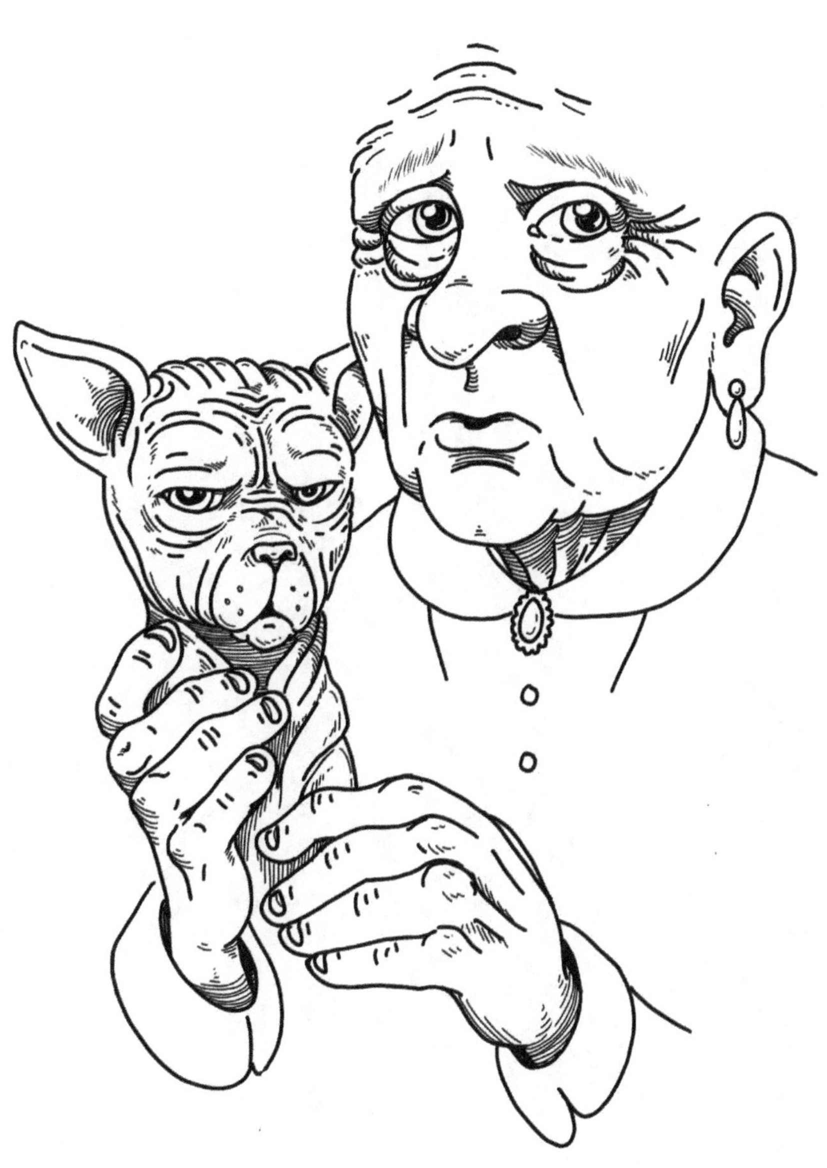

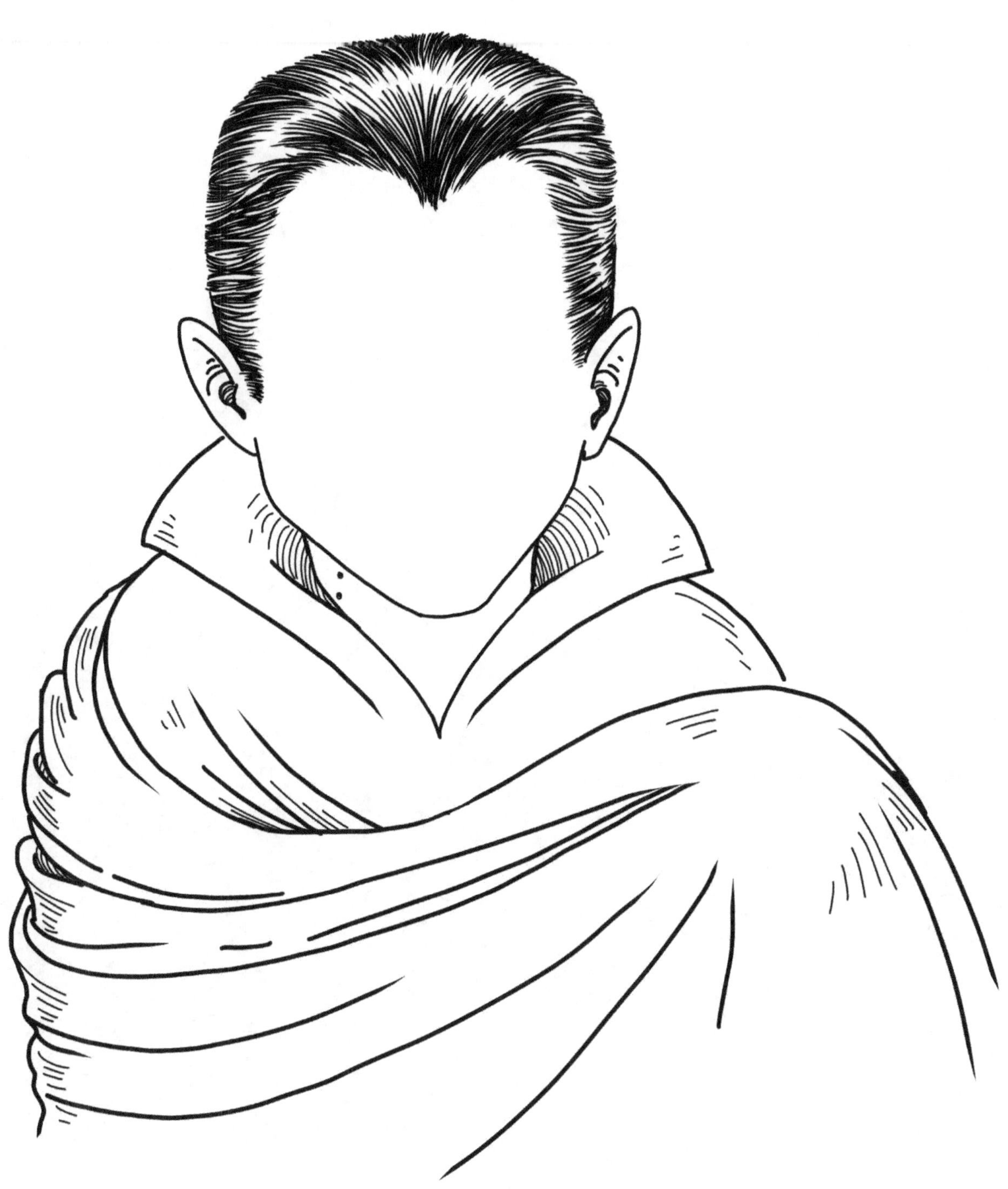

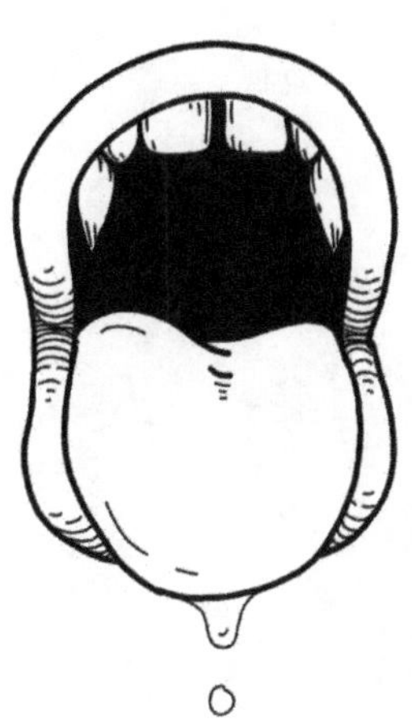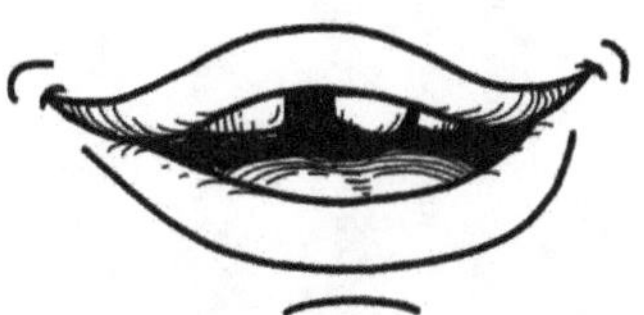

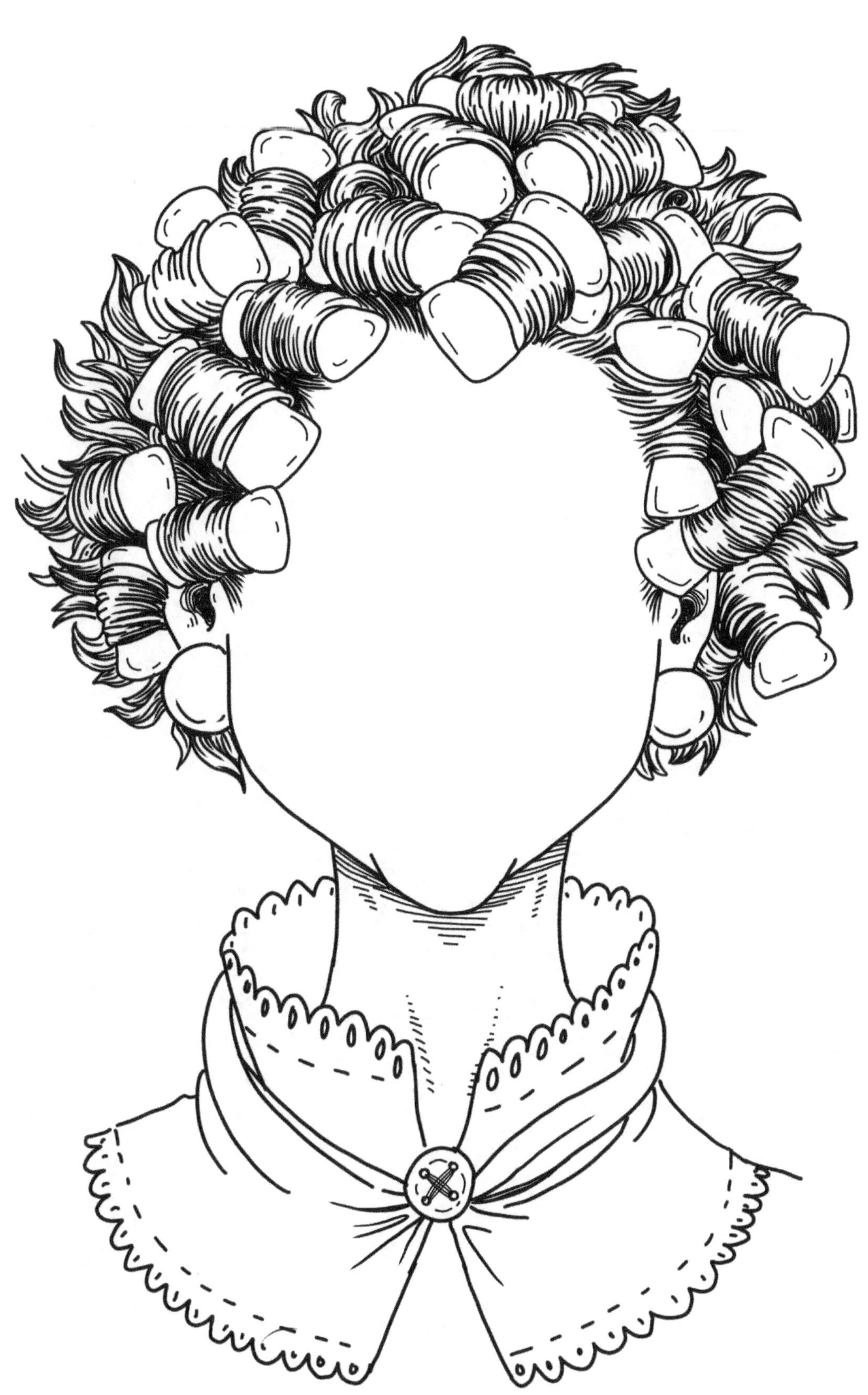

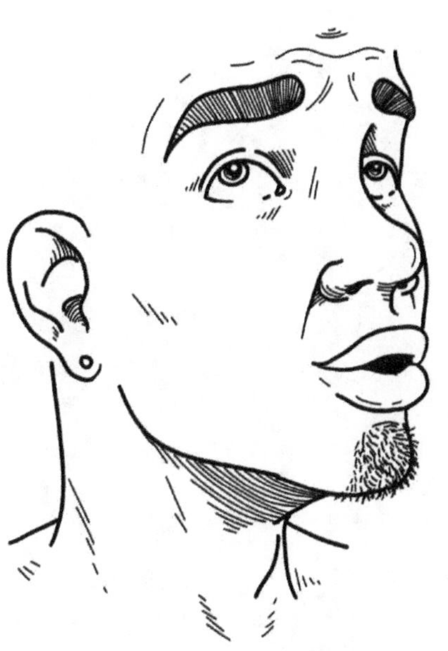

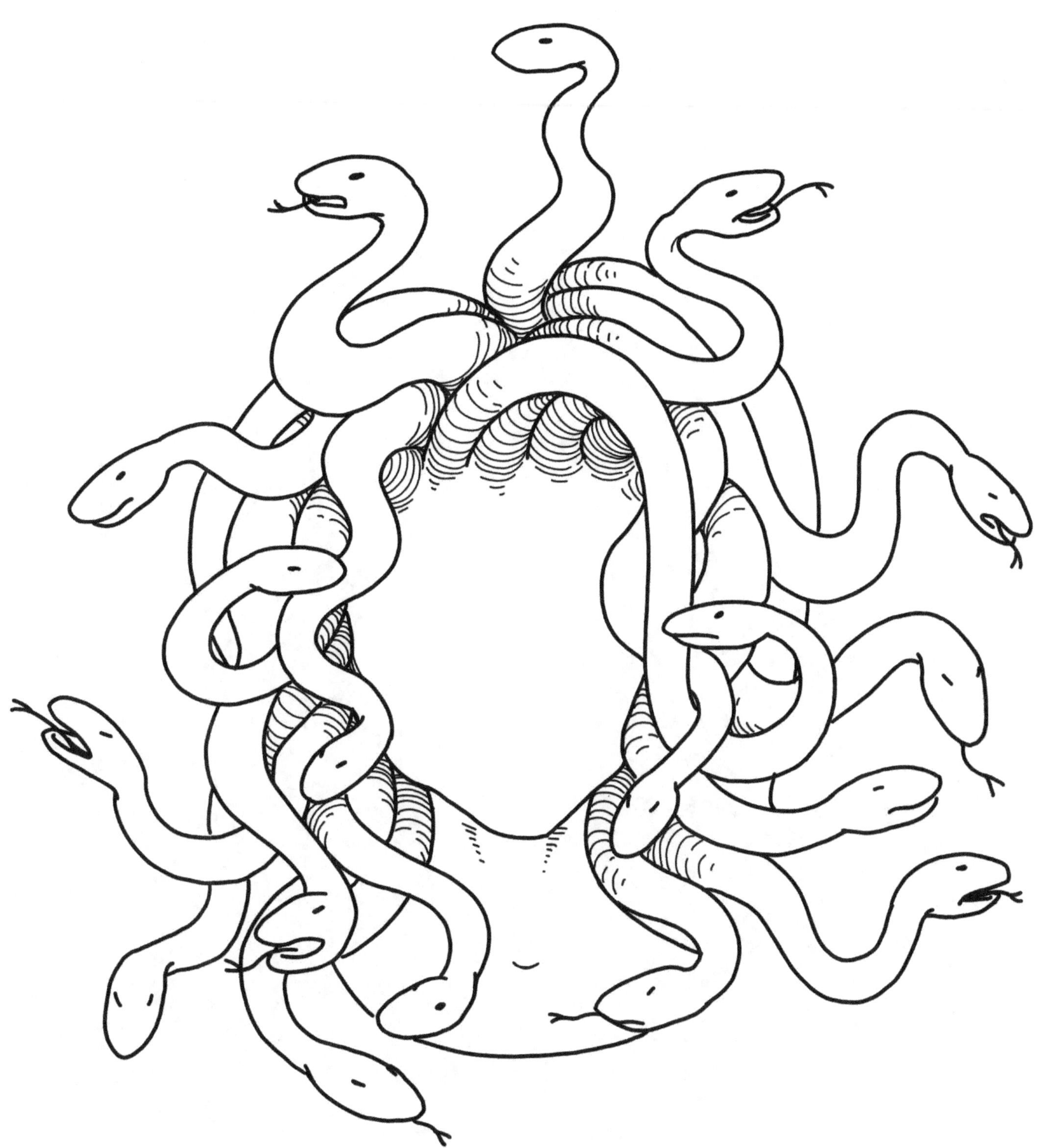

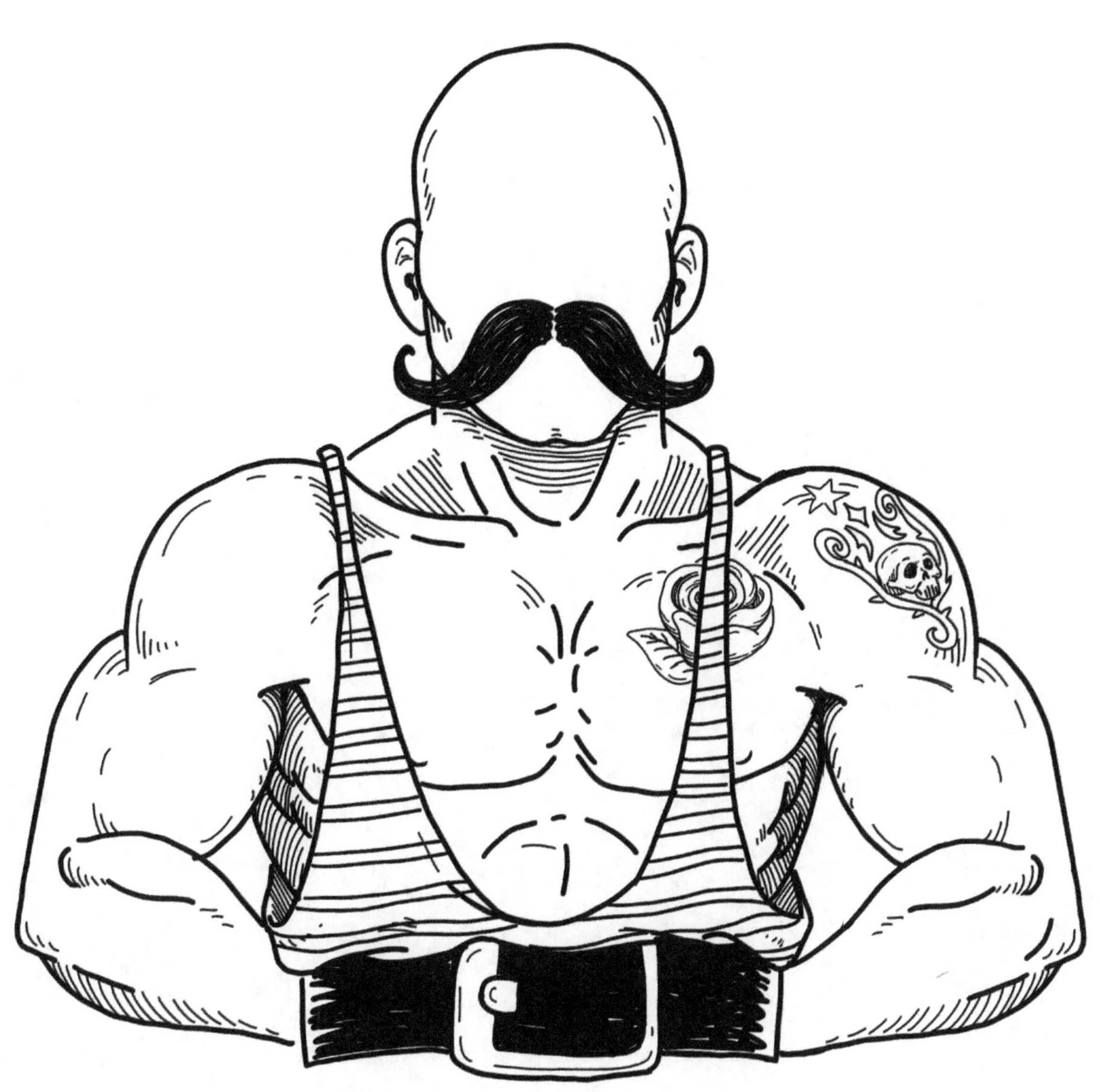

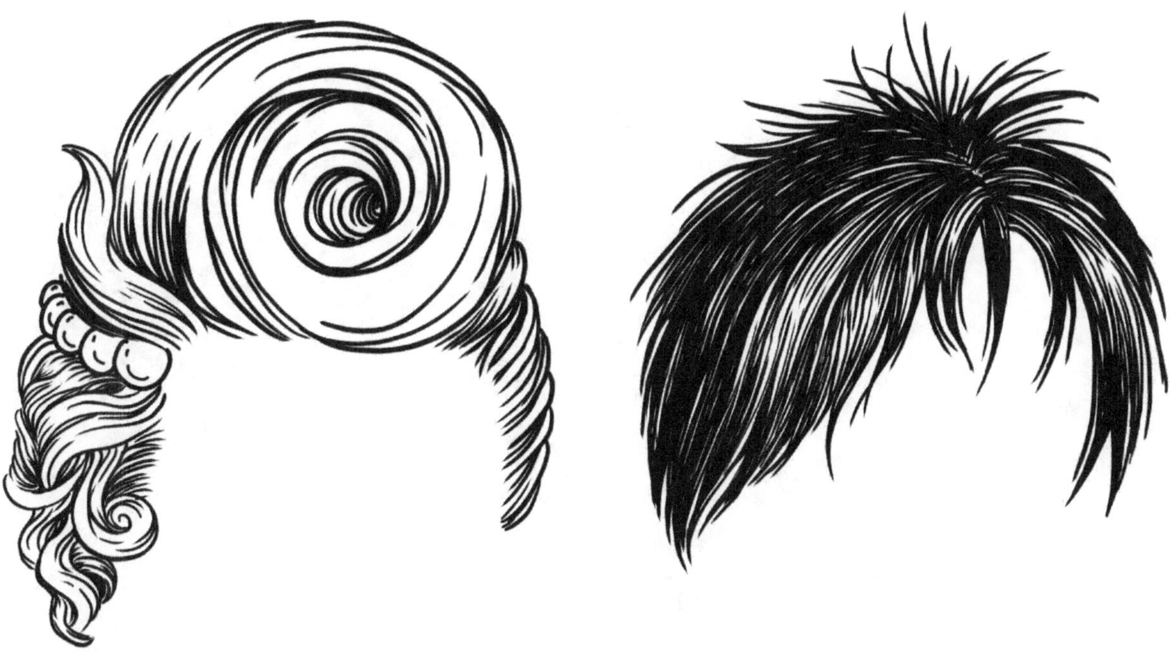

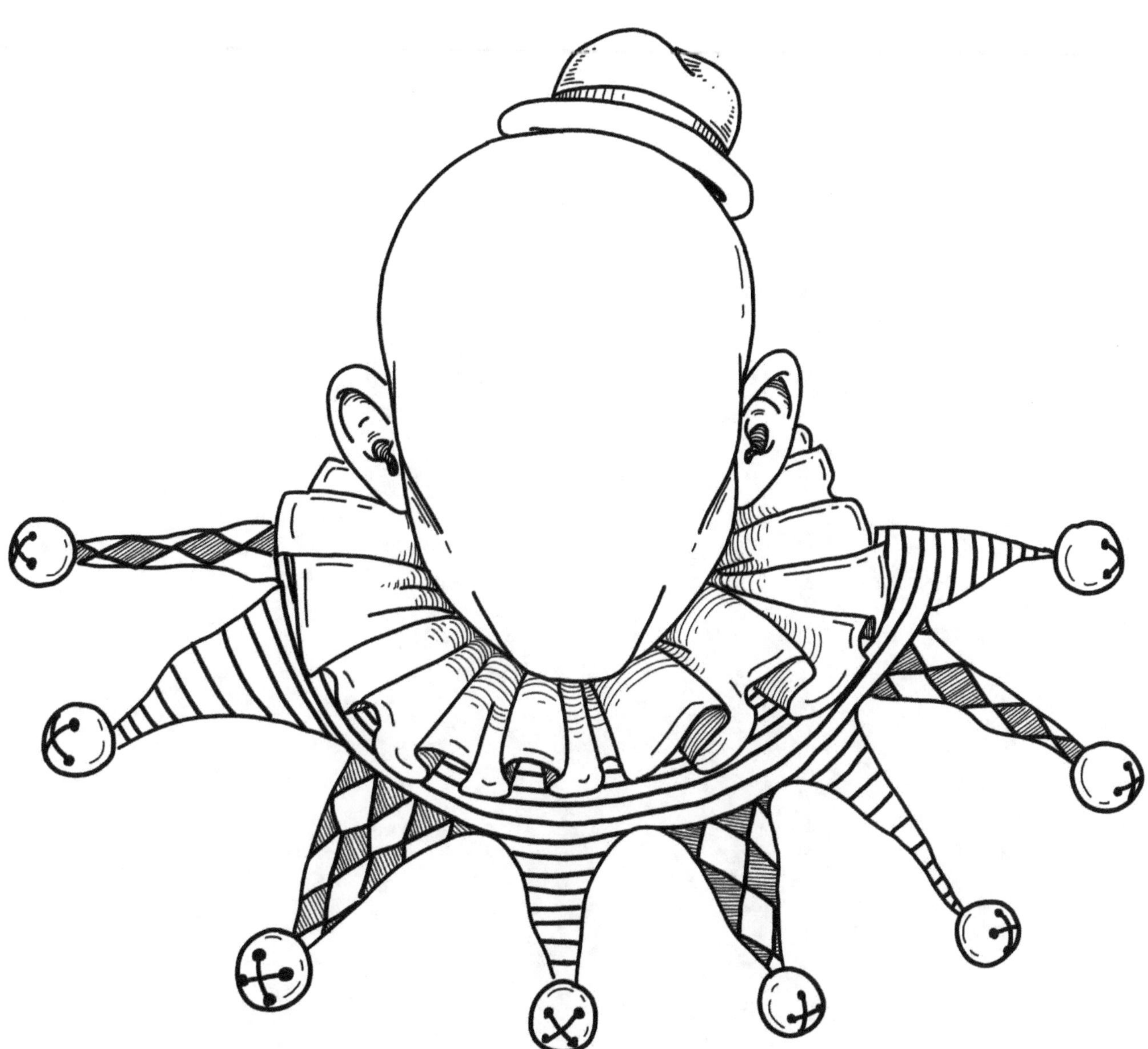

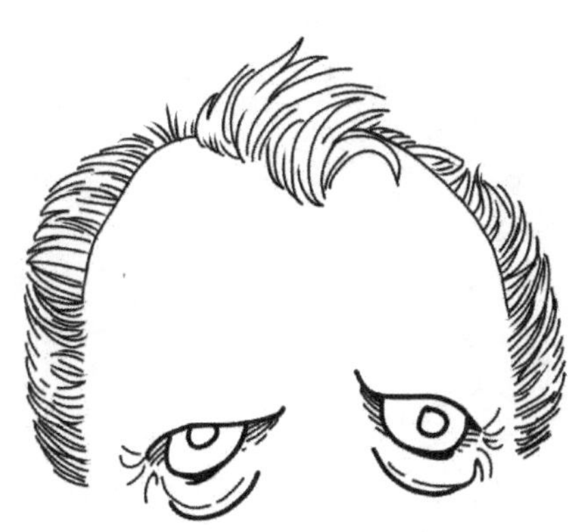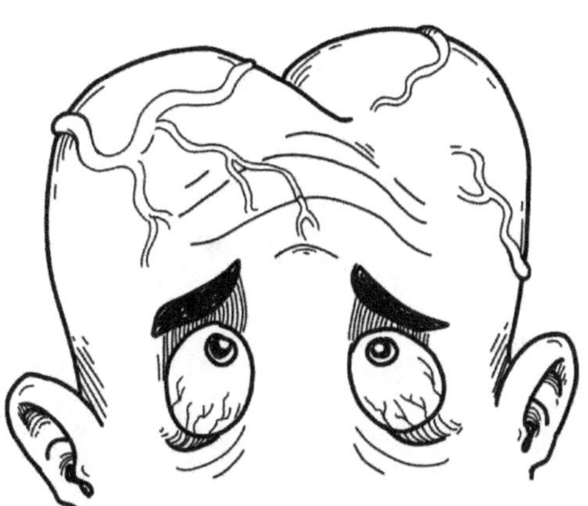

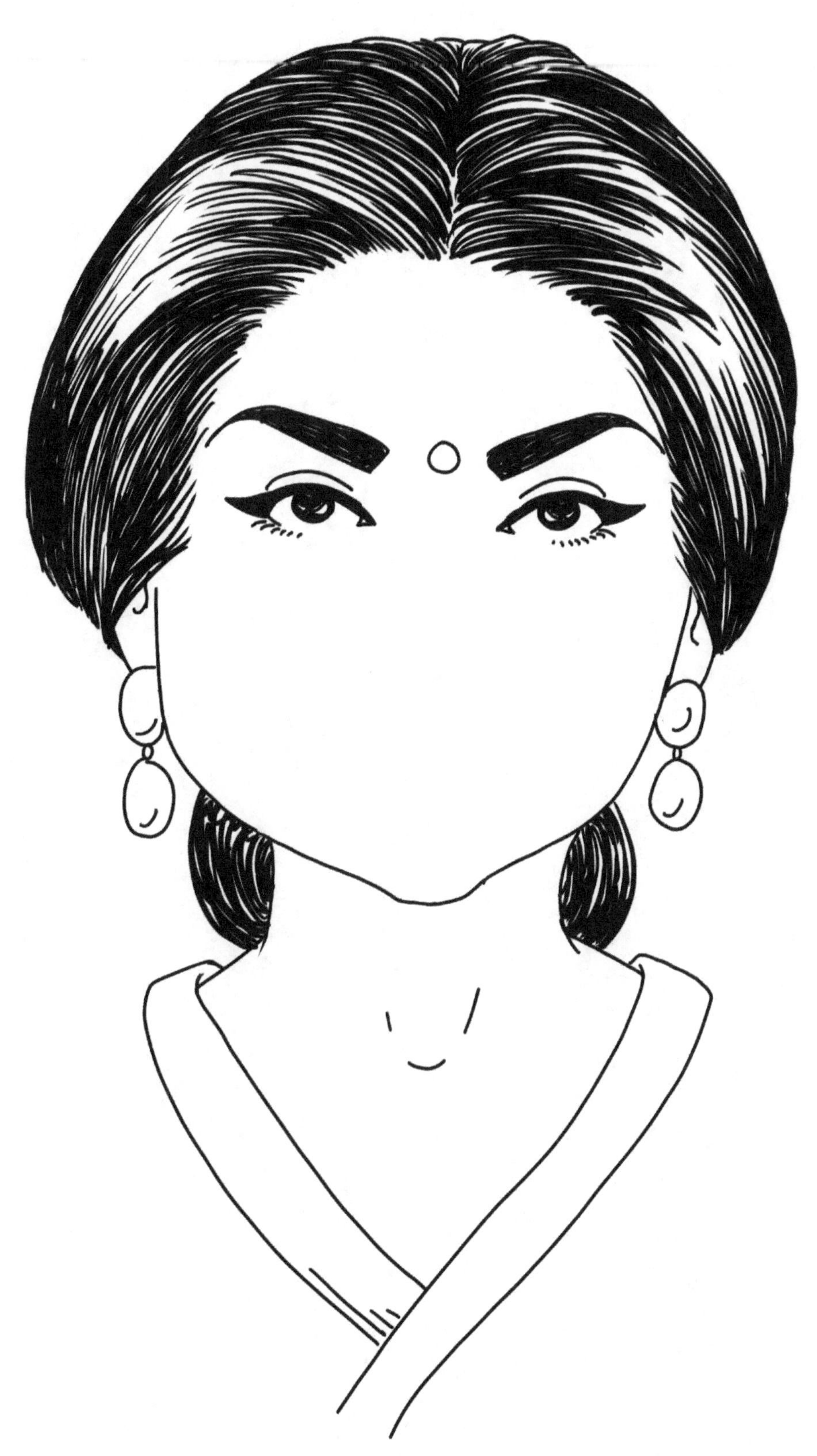

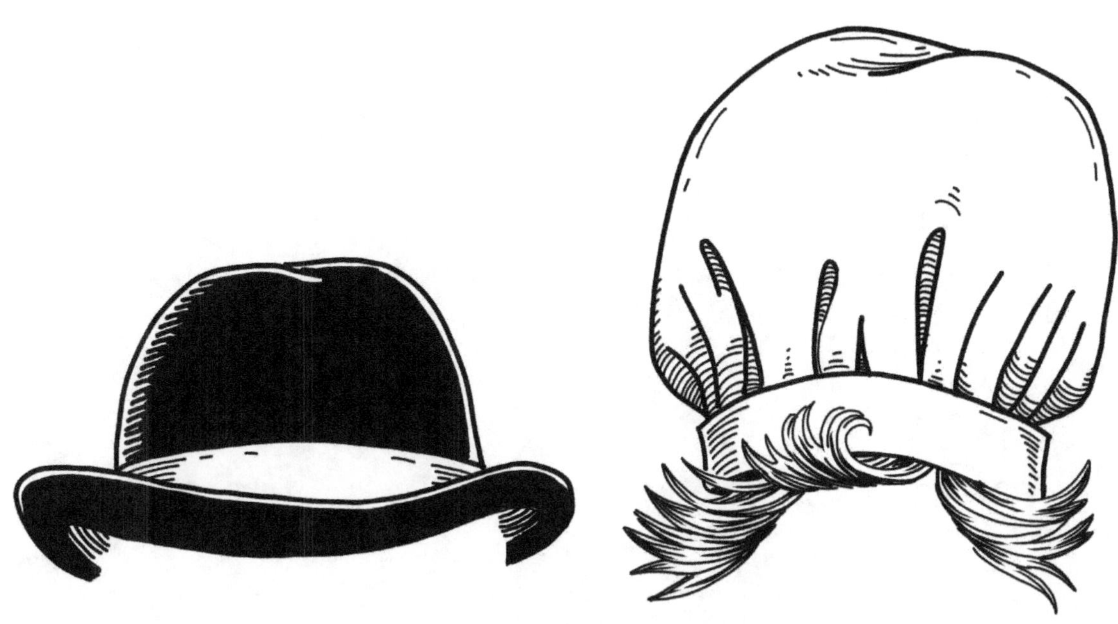

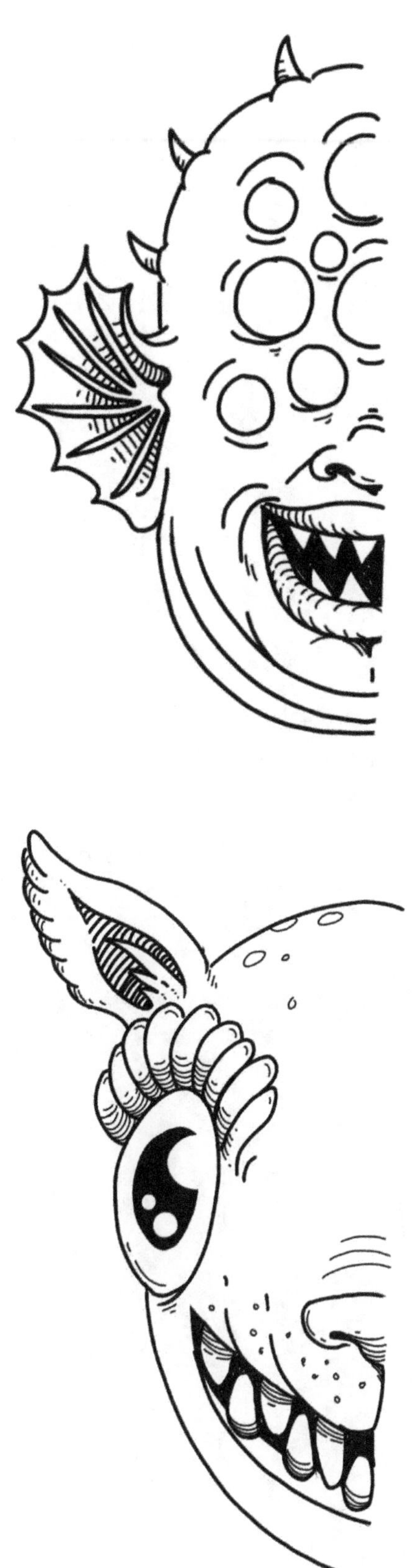

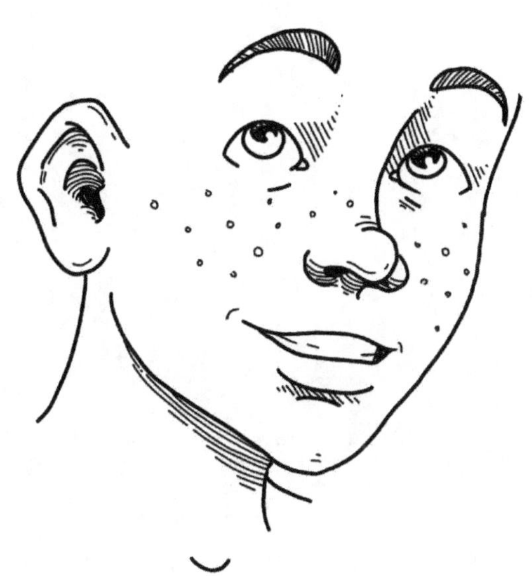

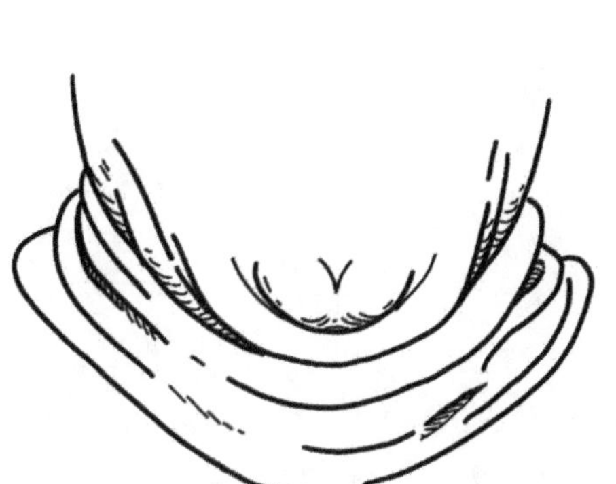

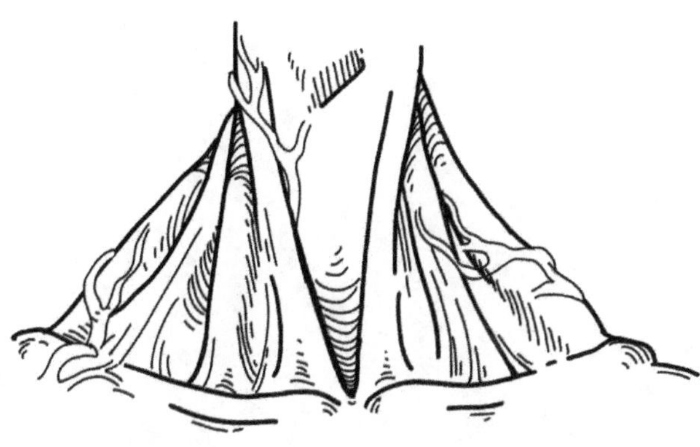

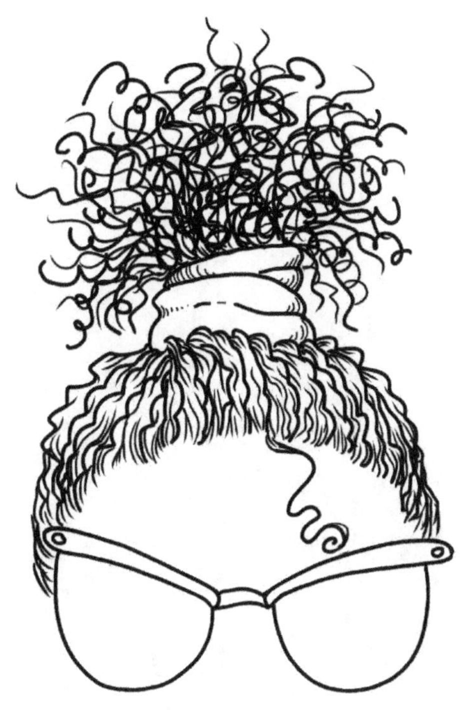

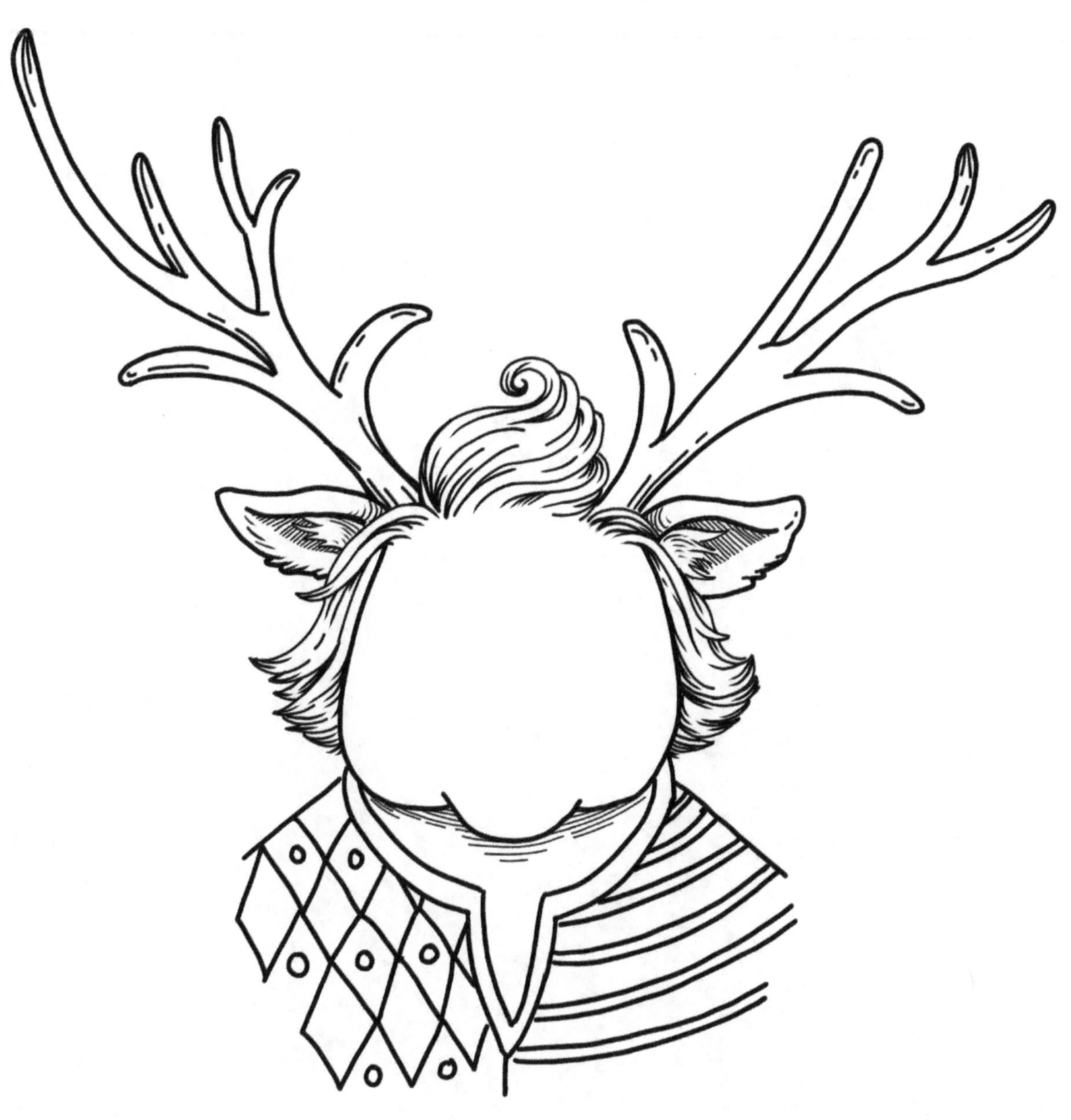

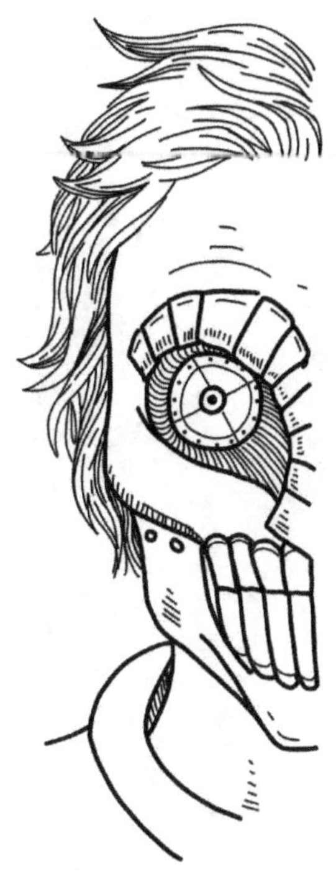

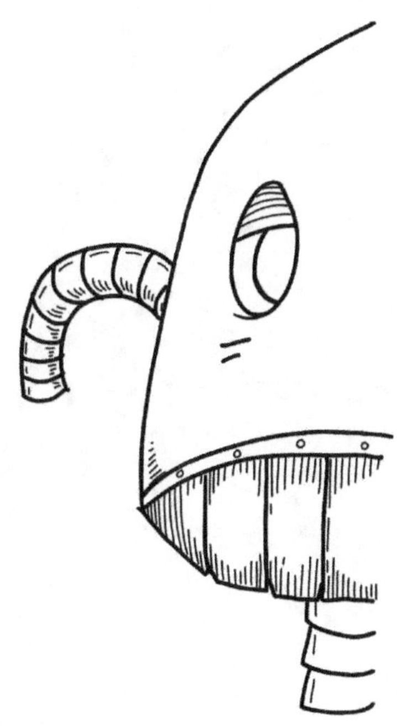

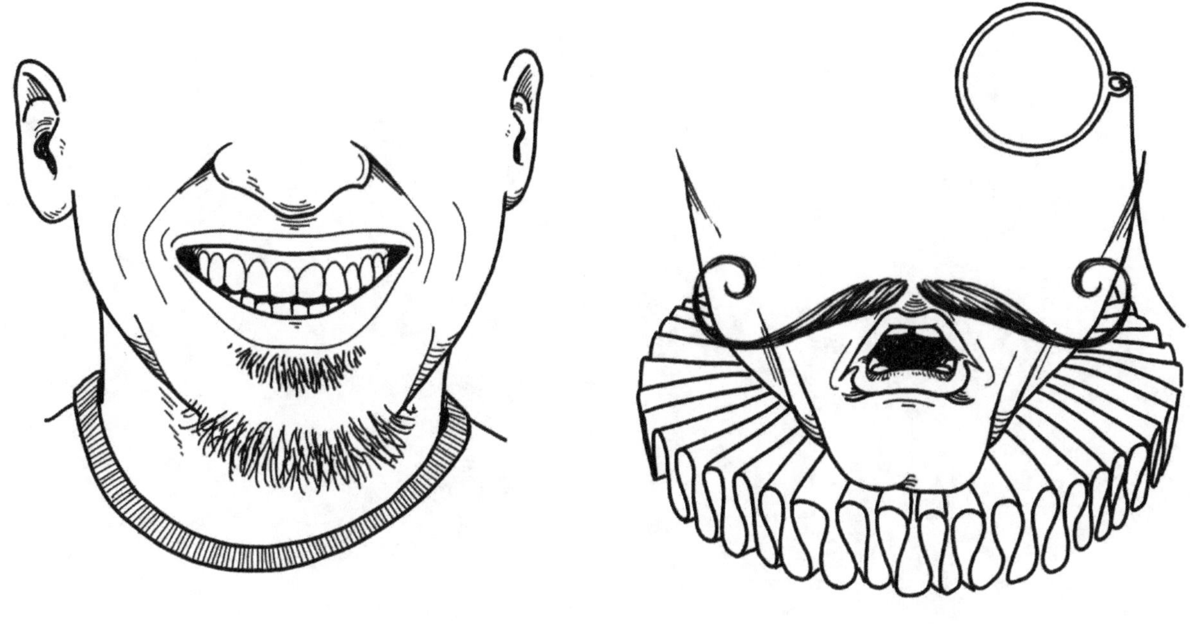

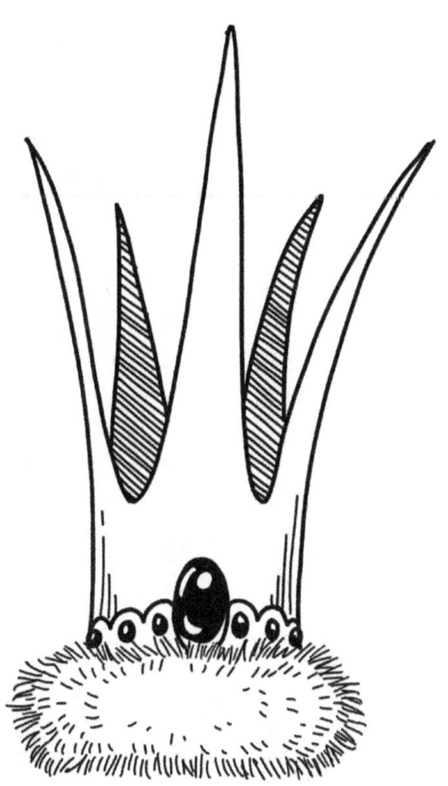
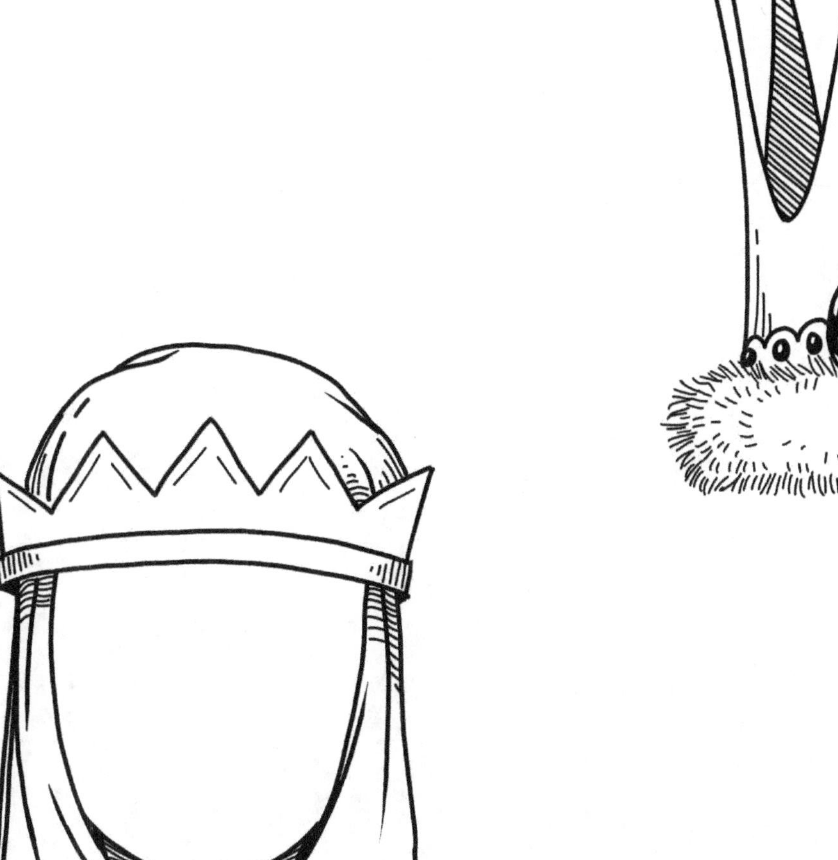

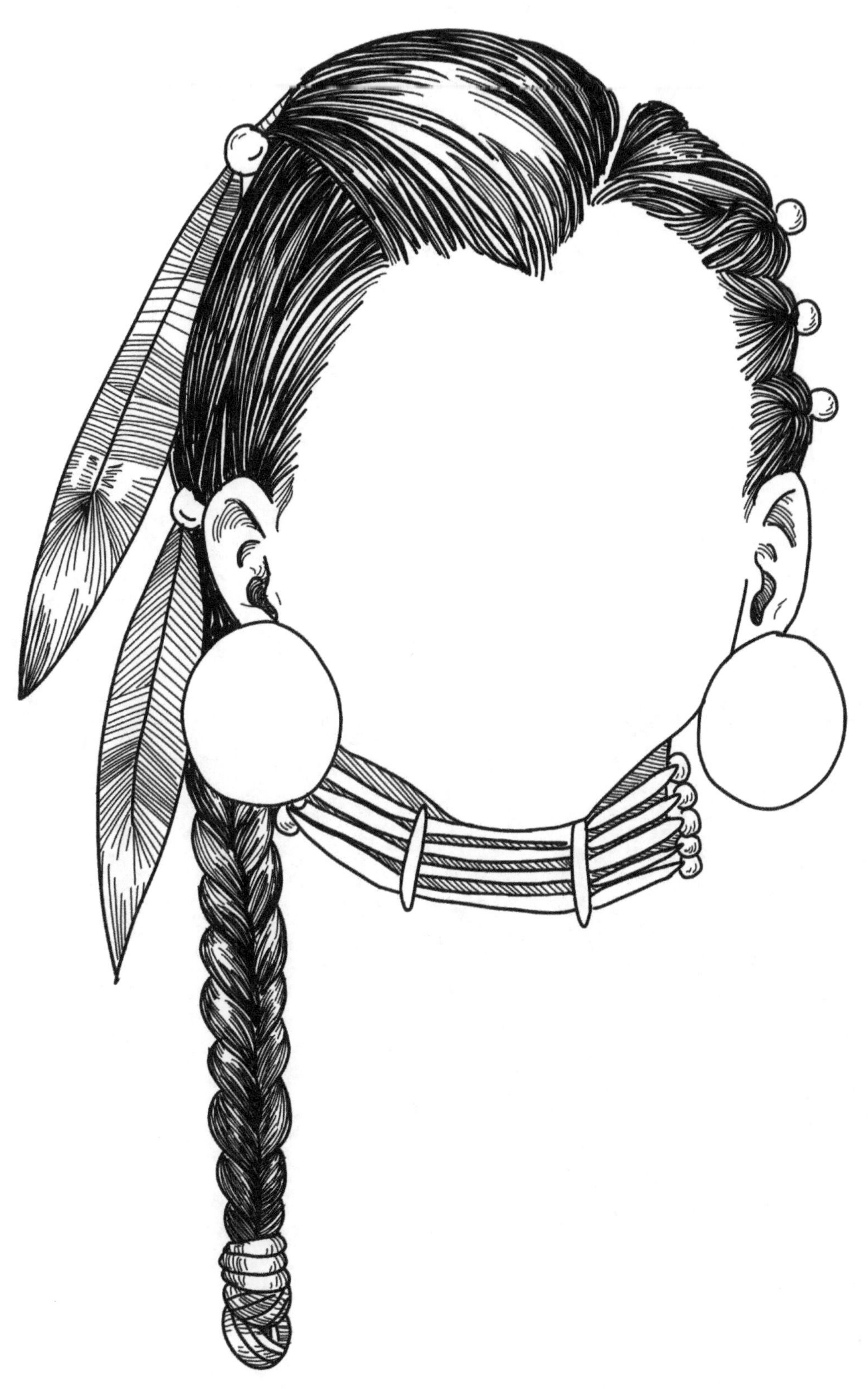

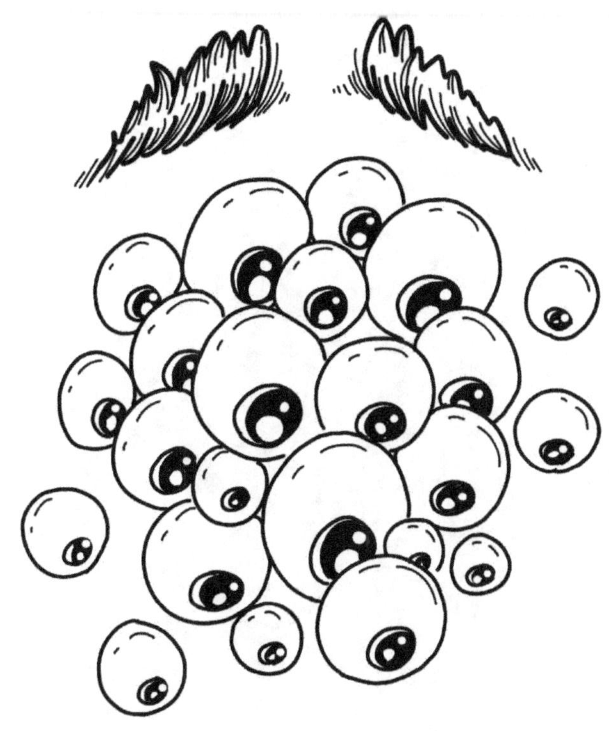

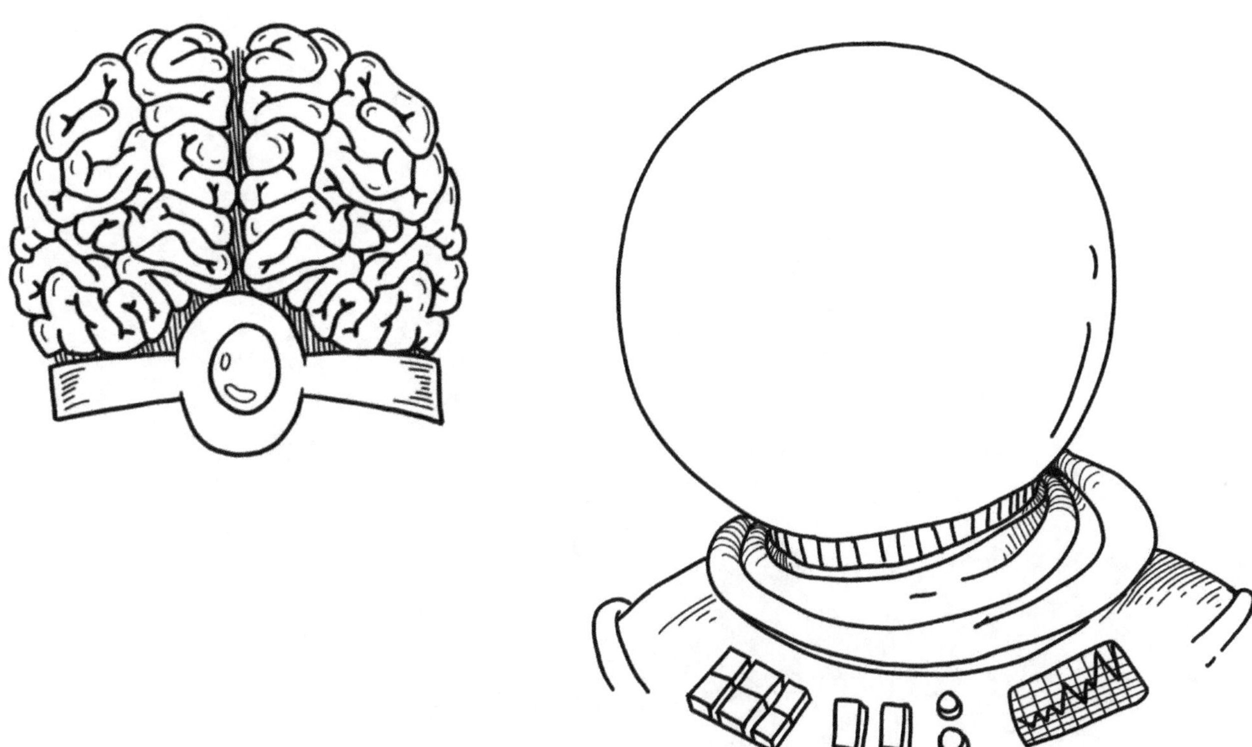

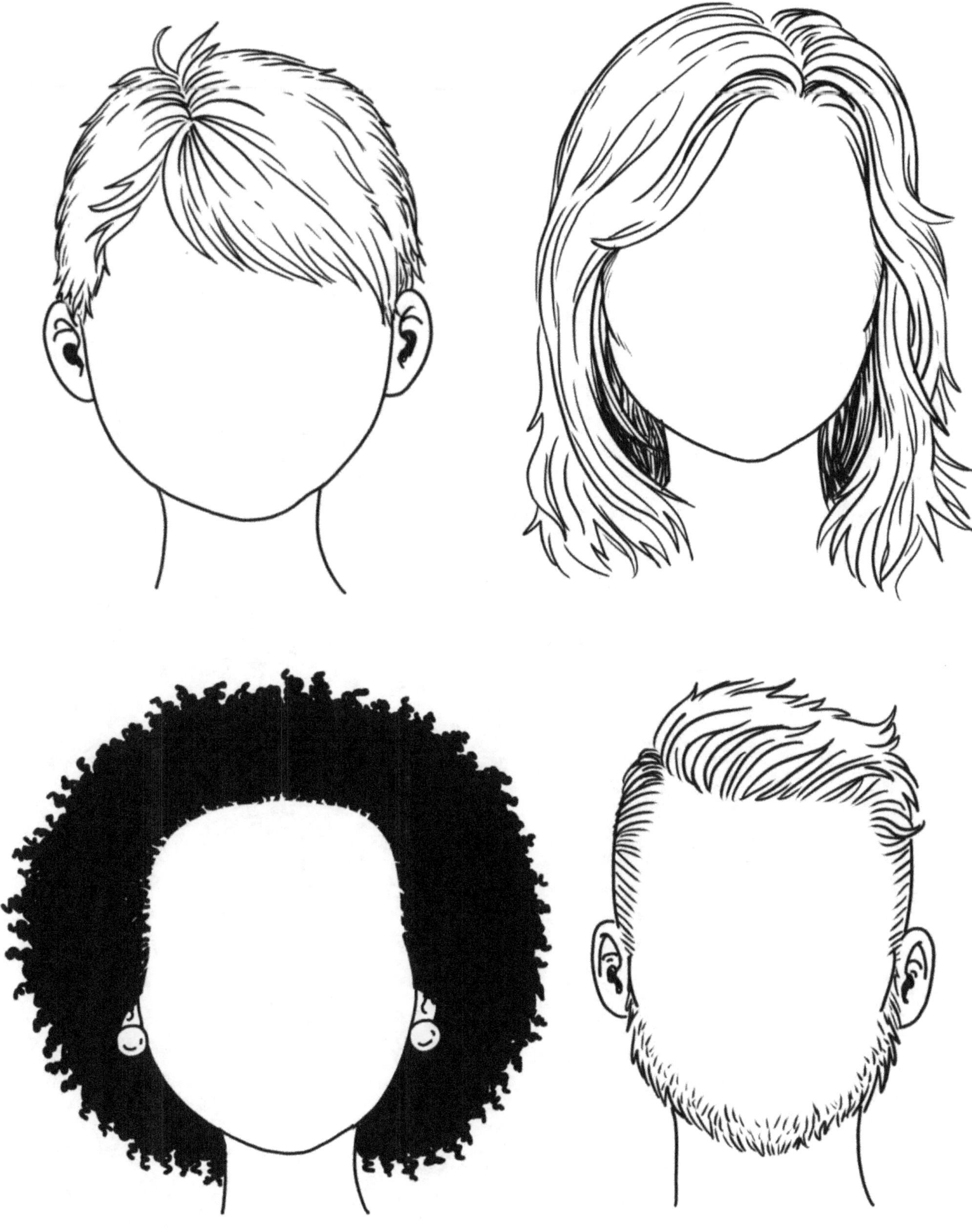

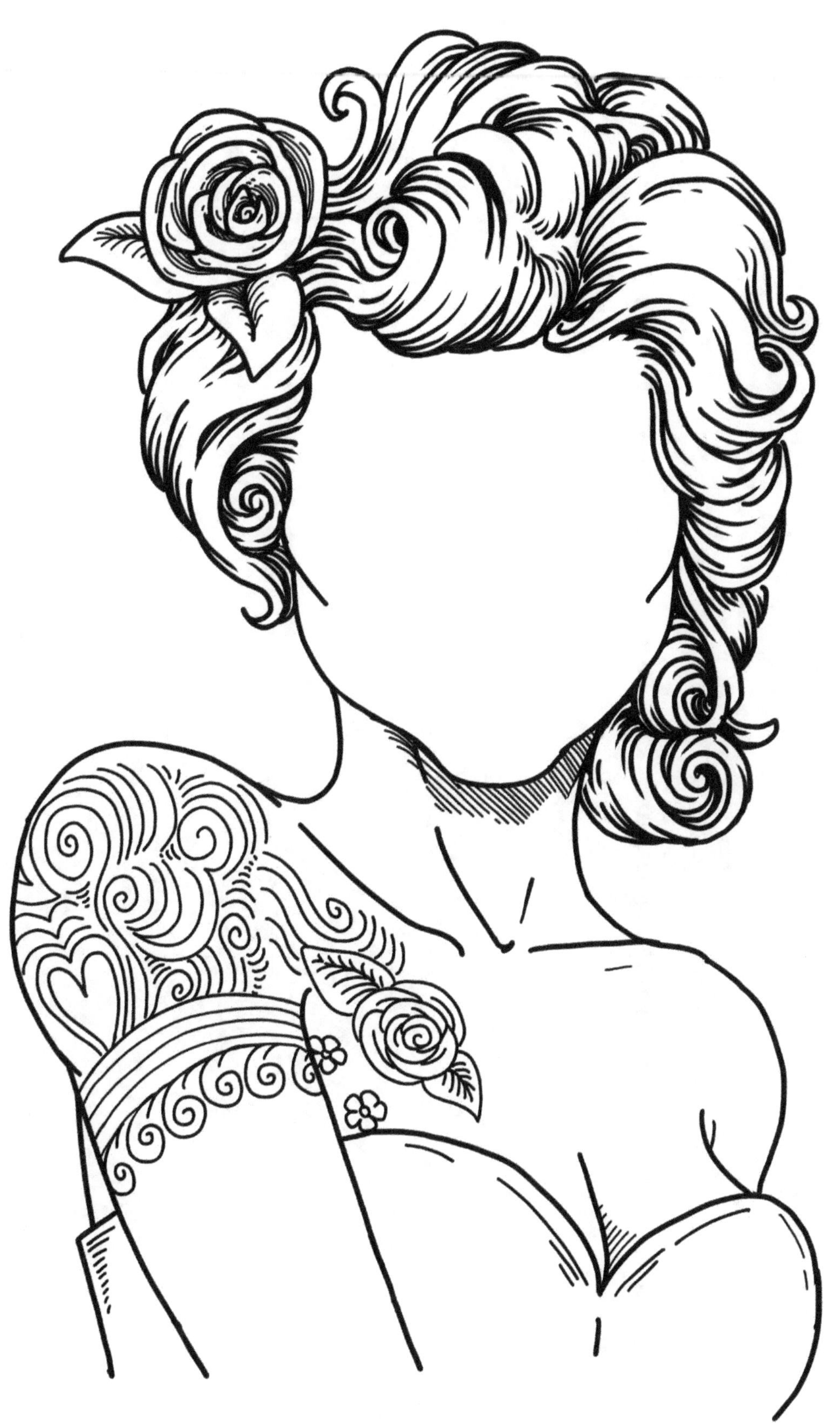

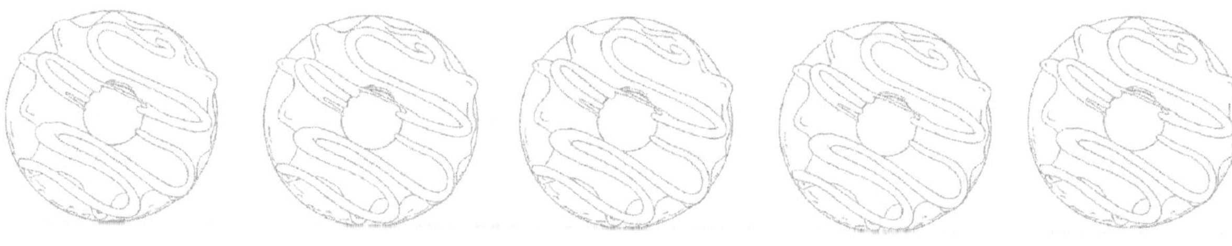

Be sure to check out Volume One...

...and Volume Two!

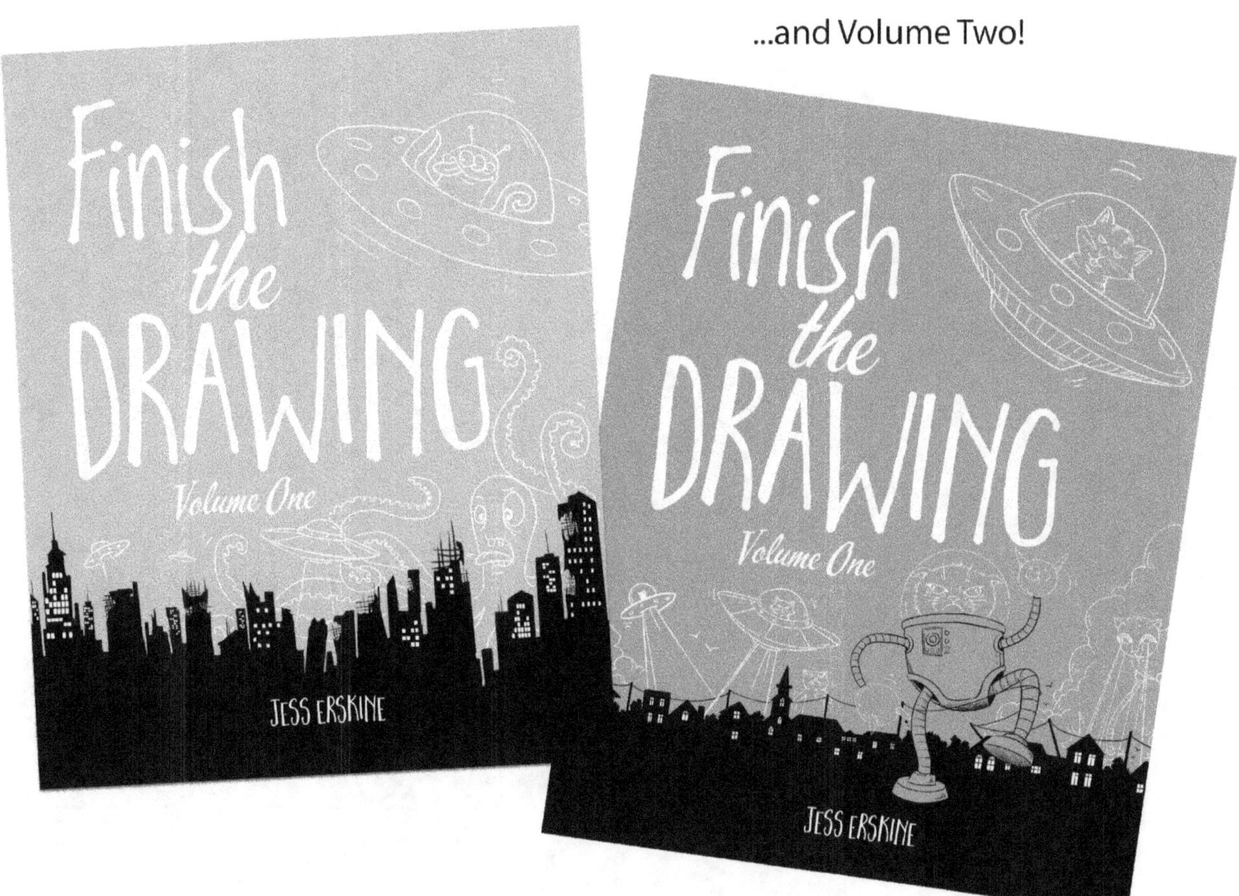

For more great titles visit us at:
www.RollingDonutPress.com

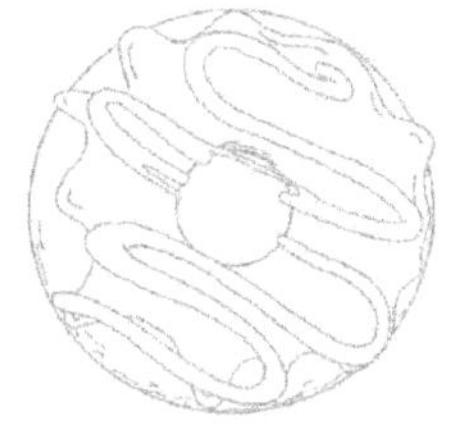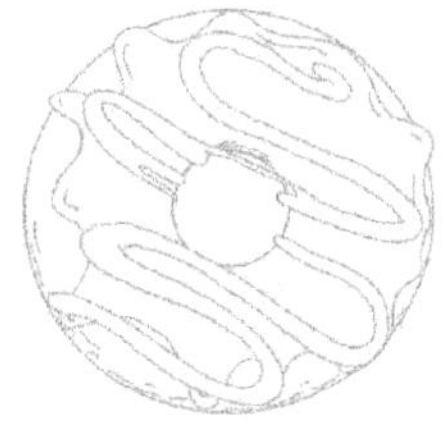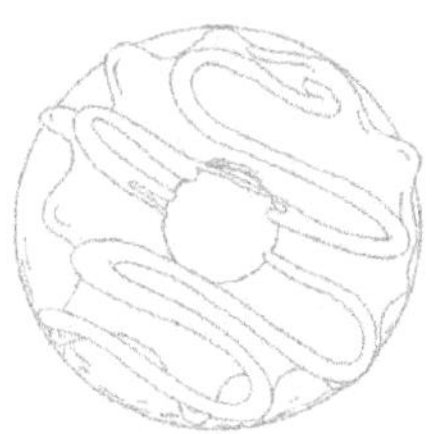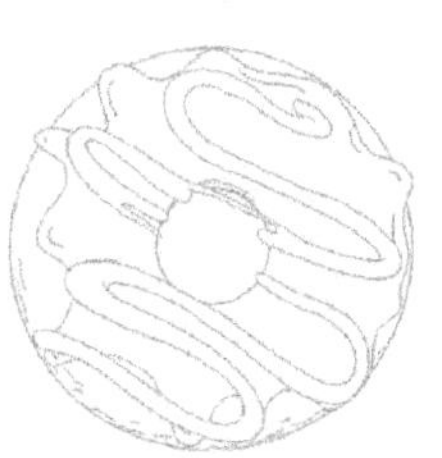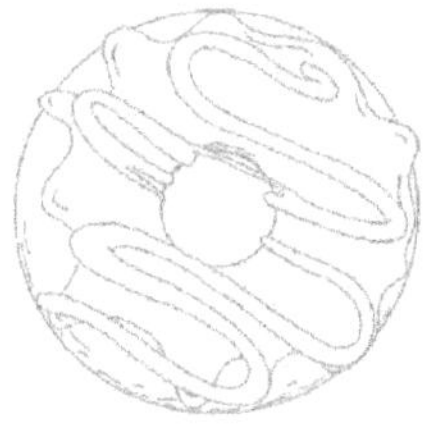

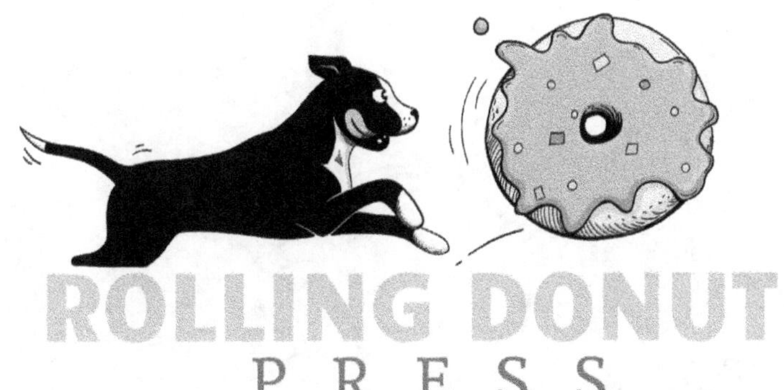

ROLLING DONUT
PRESS

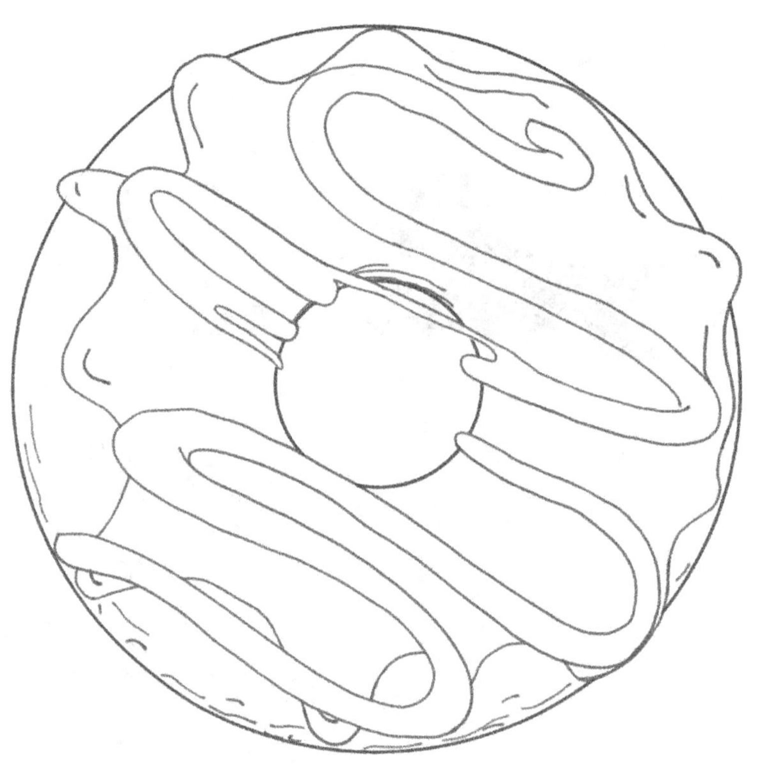